How to Enter the Presence of God

You've always yearned to—
Now here's how!

Terry Law

Victory House Publishers
Tulsa, Oklahoma

How to Enter the Presence of God
ISBN: 0-932081-39-8
Copyright © 1994 by Terry Law
P.O. Box 92, Tulsa, OK 74101

Published by:
Victory House, Inc.
P.O. Box 700238, Tulsa, OK 74170

Cover art, page design & typesetting by: Sigma Graphic Design

Table of Contents

Introduction

WITHIN EACH PERSON there is a deep desire to be in the presence of God. You may not understand it fully, you may not even be aware of it, but there's a passion in your heart to be where God is. God made you that way, and that desire is never satisfied until you are in His presence — it's a universal human need. It is basic to your happiness in life.

Man was created by God to be a worshiper. The issue is not *whether* you're going to worship, but *whom or what* you're going to worship, because you are created to be a worshiper. In the old days, people worshiped idols. They would build a golden calf or some other creature and they would bow down and worship it.

Today, men and women are still searching to find someone or something to worship. All mankind, even the worst sinner in the world, is a worshiper. He may worship money, sex, a political system, or power, but he is still a worshiper.

Ultimately he decides what to worship, but the drive inside him is the hunger to find God, to be where God is, and to worship Him.

In John 4, Jesus asked a Samaritan woman at a well to draw water for Him. She was shocked. She came during the middle of the day when all the other women were at home.

She couldn't come when the other women came to the well because she was an outcast; she was a prostitute.

When Jesus asked her for a drink, she was surprised that a Jew would ask a Samaritan, like herself, to draw water for Him. She couldn't understand this.

Then Jesus began to minister to her. He said, "Go and get your husband."

She said, "I don't have a husband."

Supernaturally, Jesus knew many things about the woman. He said, "You have rightly said that you don't have a husband. You've had five husbands and the man you're living with now is not your husband."

Again, she was shocked. She said, "Sir, I perceive that you are a prophet."

Jesus knew that sexual immorality was not the answer to that woman's problem. She was jumping from husband to husband, from bed to bed, because she thought that sex was the answer to the desire she had inside.

Mankind does not understand that sex will not fulfill the longing and desire we experience deep in our hearts. Money is not the answer either. Power is not the answer. Only when you meet God do you find an answer to that longing inside. Only when you worship Him and sit in His presence are you truly content. Only then is that hunger for fellowship, the hunger to be with God, satisfied.

Jesus knew that sex was not meeting the Samaritan woman's need. He knew that it couldn't satisfy her. But He didn't rebuke her. He didn't say, "Woman, you're a great sinner. How could you consort with all those men?" He didn't say that. He knew what her real problem was.

He said, *"But the hour cometh, and now is, when the true worshippers shall worship* [not men, not immorality, but they shall worship] *the Father in spirit and in truth: for the Father seeketh such to worship him"* (John 4:23).

That is a powerful statement. Think about it. *The Father seeks you to worship Him.* Let me say that again: the Father seeks you to worship Him. There is something in the heart of God that is seeking after you. God wants you to worship Him. He wants you to fellowship with Him. He wants to be to you what He was to Adam and Eve, walking in the Garden of Eden. That's what is in the heart of God.

When God originally created Adam and Eve, He had fellowship with them every day. They had communion together: they were in His presence. He would come in the cool of the evening and walk in the Garden with them. That was the original plan of God for the human race. That's the way we were created to live: in fellowship with God.

Sin has separated mankind from God; yet God still desires our fellowship. That is a mystery to us, but the Word states it as an indisputable fact. After Adam and Eve sinned and went their own way, God immediately instituted a plan for getting mankind back to the place where they could walk in fellowship with Him once again.

Every believer desires that fellowship and wants to have a powerful daily devotional time, but they don't know how to come into the presence of God. They are hounded by a sense of guilt. God seems so far away. Devotional times seem dry and laborious.

This book explains how to enter into His presence. It will create an "I want to" and "I can't wait" inside you. The pattern God uses to show us how to enter His presence is in the Tabernacle of Moses.

This is probably the most important and powerful teaching the Lord has given me. I practice these principles as a part of my own devotional life. They have literally transformed my approach to God.

When you enter God's presence, something special happens. Not only do you experience worship and fellowship, but you begin to receive revelation. You'll see powerful, spiritual truth — not dry, religious doctrine, but spiritually alive truth that will get you healed and blessed in your marriage, your family, and your finances.

Some of us have been Christians for ten years, fifteen years, twenty years, some even thirty years or longer. As you read this book and follow the Holy Spirit's teachings on the Tabernacle of Moses, you will come into a relationship and intimacy with God, the Father, like you've never known before in your life! In His presence, you will experience "fullness of joy"!

1

Why the Tabernacle of Moses?

FROM THE BEGINNING, God has wanted mankind to worship Him and come into His presence. The passion of His heart is to be with us. Think about it! God wants to be with you! And we desire to come to Him. But how can we approach God, who is so awesome and majestic?

IN THE OLD TESTAMENT, God designed a way for Moses and the Israelites to come into His presence. He made a way so that the glory of God could dwell among men.

The children of Israel knew that God was interested in them because they saw the miracles He did on their behalf: the plagues of Egypt that finally persuaded Pharaoh to release them from slavery, and the opening of the Red Sea that helped them escape from the Egyptian army. They saw God's mighty works, but they didn't know how to get to where God was. In fact, they were afraid of God. His presence frightened them.

The presence of God in the Old Testament was known as the *Shekinah,* and it was a pillar of cloud by day and a pillar of fire by night. Man could not come anywhere near God's

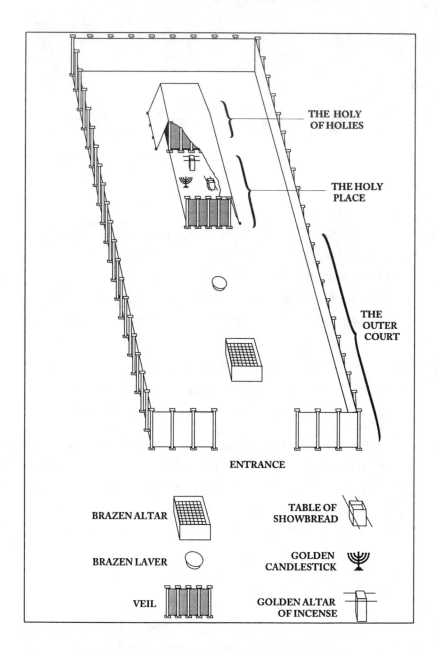

THE HOLY
OF HOLIES

THE HOLY
PLACE

THE
OUTER
COURT

ENTRANCE

BRAZEN ALTAR	TABLE OF SHOWBREAD
BRAZEN LAVER	GOLDEN CANDLESTICK
VEIL	GOLDEN ALTAR OF INCENSE

THE TABERNACLE OF MOSES
(with cut-away view of the Holy Place)

presence, because if a man got too close to the presence of God, he would be struck dead.

The Tabernacle of Moses

God called one of the Israelites up to the top of a mountain. His name was Moses. God said, "Moses, I'm going to show you how to come into my presence. I'm going to give you a plan and a pattern so you can walk into my presence. We're going to call it the Tabernacle."

The Tabernacle of Moses is the greatest, Holy Spirit-given pattern in the entire Bible for how to come into the presence of God. And the Holy Spirit has confirmed the Tabernacle as God's plan and God's outline for the Church, to show New Testament believers how we are to come into His presence, as well.

That's why so much of the Bible speaks about the Tabernacle. Did you know that in the Old Testament there are over fifty chapters that refer to it? And in the New Testament book of Hebrews, 131 of its 303 verses, or forty-three percent of the entire book, deal with the Tabernacle. Yet, when you ask the average Christian, "What do you know about the Tabernacle of Moses?" most believers don't know anything about it!

Let's look closely at the following passage from the Scriptures:

Now the first covenant *[the Old Testament]* **had regulations** *[or rites]* **for worship and also an earthly sanctuary** *[or a church, a tabernacle]*. **A tabernacle was set up. In its first room were the lampstand** *[or candlestick]*, **the table and the**

consecrated bread *[or showbread]*; this was called the Holy Place. Behind the second curtain [or veil] was a room called the Most Holy Place *[or the Holy of Holies]*, which had the golden altar of incense and the gold-covered ark of the covenant. This ark contained the gold jar of manna, Aaron's staff that had budded, and the stone tablets of the covenant. Above the ark were the cherubim of the Glory, overshadowing the atonement cover *[also called the mercy seat]*. But we cannot discuss these things in detail now. When everything had been arranged like this, the priests entered regularly into the outer room *[into the Holy Place]*, to carry on their ministry. But only the high priest entered the inner room *[into the area called the Holy of Holies]*, and that only once a year, and never without blood, which he offered for himself and for the sins the people had committed in ignorance. The Holy Spirit was showing by this that the way into the Most Holy Place had not yet been disclosed as long as the first tabernacle was still standing.

(Heb. 9:1-8, NIV)

Note that in verse 7, the high priest went into the presence of God on behalf of the people. He represented the people there, but he didn't dare go on his own. He had to go in with blood, and he offered that blood for himself, and for the sin, or the errors, of the people.

A Pattern for Christians

Now let's examine verse 8. The Holy Spirit is saying that the way into the Holy of Holies (the Most Holy Place) was not yet opened or made manifest while the first tabernacle was still standing. There *is* a way into the presence of God, but it's not the Old Testament way. Rather, the Old Testament way is a *pattern* of the New Testament way.

Hebrews 8:5-6 makes this very clear.

They serve at a sanctuary *[tabernacle]* **that is a copy and shadow of what is in heaven. This is why Moses was warned when he was about to build the tabernacle: "See to it that you make everything according to the pattern shown you on the mountain."** (NIV)

These verses tell us that the Tabernacle is a pattern, a copy or a shadow, of what heaven is really like. If you want to understand the presence of God in heaven, then study the pattern of the Tabernacle.

Hebrews 9:8 indicates that the Holy Spirit was showing us by the Tabernacle that there is a way into the Holy of Holies. That's good news, friends! There is a way to come into God's presence.

If we will follow the Holy Spirit's teaching on the Tabernacle, He will show us how to come into the very presence of the holiness of God and not be smitten dead. When we get into that place where the holiness of God is, healing comes naturally. We will come into fellowship, we'll come into relationship, we'll come into blessing in every way, we'll come into the place where the power of God is so awesome and so beautiful and so majestic that nothing we've ever experienced before in our Christian lives can compare with being where God is.

In Hebrews 10:19, the Holy Spirit says:

> **Therefore, brothers,** *[He's talking to believers]* **since we have confidence to enter the Most Holy Place** *[there is an invitation for you and me to come boldly into the Holy of Holies. How do we do it?]*, **by the blood of Jesus....**

So there is a way to come into the Holy of Holies; there is a way to be in the presence and power of God. There is a way that you can see signs and wonders and miracles happening every day of your life. There is a hallowed place where you can experience complete joy. God tells us, *"Come in. I want you here."* And He gives us a step-by-step plan to follow.

The Outer Court and the Holy Places

The Tabernacle of Moses had three parts. If you would have walked up to the Tabernacle and looked at it from the outside, all you would have seen was a seven-and-a-half-foot white linen fence running all the way around the Tabernacle. That's all you could have seen. It would have been 150 feet long on two sides, and seventy-five feet wide on the other two sides. This seven-and-a-half-foot high linen fence enclosed something called "the outer court."

(Now in Herod's temple, the outer court was called "Solomon's Porch." That is where Peter and John came and raised the lame man who was sitting at the gate. He was sitting at the gate of Solomon's Porch, or the outer court.)

Inside this white linen curtain was a tent-like building that the Israelites could carry through the wilderness with them. This building had two compartments. The first one was called the Holy Place, and it was separated from the second compartment by a thick curtain or veil. The second area was called the Holy of Holies, or the place where the presence of God dwelt. The actual glory of God dwelt in a cloud over the mercy seat on the Ark of the Covenant. So you have the three areas: the outer court, the Holy Place, and the Holy of Holies.

When you walked into the outer court, you could see the portable building, but the priests were the only ones who were allowed into the second area, or the Holy Place. And the high priest was the only one who once a year was allowed into the Holy of Holies, into the very presence of God.

(It is interesting to note that the priests went into the Holy Place every afternoon at precisely 3:00 and there they made the evening sacrifice. It was called "the time of the evening oblation." Now Jesus Christ died on the cross and gave up the ghost at precisely 3:00 in the afternoon as well. So we know that there were priests standing in front of the veil when Jesus cried out and gave up the ghost. The priests watched as God rent the veil in two from the top to the bottom at precisely 3:00, when Jesus said, "It is finished." Isn't it amazing how accurately and precisely God does His work?)

Our Outer Court and Holy Places

There is a powerful comparison between the three areas of the Tabernacle and you as a person. The Bible says, in 1 Thessalonians 5:23, *"May God himself, the God of peace, sanc-*

tify you through and through. May your whole spirit, soul and body be kept blameless at the coming of our Lord Jesus Christ" (NIV).

Notice we have three parts: we are spirit, soul, and body. All people recognize they have a body. Many realize they have a soul, but few acknowledge their spirit. Your body, however, is just the outward shell. The real you is your spirit. You are a spirit, you have a soul, and you live in a body.

Your body has five senses: touch, taste, smell, sight, and hearing. These five senses enable you to experience the world around you. With your body you are *world-conscious*.

Your soul is comprised of intelligence, will power, and emotion. You are aware of yourself as a unique creation of God through your soul. With your soul you are *self-conscious*.

Our third component is spirit. This is by far the most important part of man. God is a Spirit. They that worship Him, must worship Him in spirit and in truth. You don't comprehend God by body or soul. You experience God through the new birth in your spirit. With your spirit you are *God-conscious*.

These three parts of you as a person relate directly to the Tabernacle. Your body is the outer court. Your mind or your soul is the Holy Place. And your spirit is the Holy of Holies.

God is a Spirit and they that worship Him must worship Him in spirit and in truth. You don't worship God in your mind. If you don't know how to worship God in your spirit, then you don't really *know* God. You must learn to move from the outer court (your body), to the Holy Place (your soul), to the Holy of Holies (your spirit), because God exists in the spirit realm.

The Three Steps of Approach

There are three levels of approach to God: thanksgiving, praise, and worship. These also correspond directly to the three areas of the Tabernacle. The outer court represents thanksgiving. The Holy Place represents praise, and the Holy of Holies represents worship. This reveals the pattern of how to come into the presence of God. You begin to enter God's presence with thanksgiving. You graduate on to praise, and then you come into the ultimate *Shekinah* of God through worship. Each one is a progressive step that leads to the next. I want you to see this because it is so powerful.

A Rainbow of Worship

In understanding thanksgiving, praise, and worship, it is vital that you understand that all three elements are different. Thanksgiving is different from praise, and praise is different from worship. We could be very technical and try to divide up thanksgiving and praise and worship. In doing so, however, we might become so technical about it that we would lose the essence of the message.

When you look at a rainbow, you will see the primary colors of the rainbow, but you'll also see a lot of in-between colors as you shade from one primary color into the next. There's a moving from red to orange to yellow, and from yellow to green to blue. That's the way a rainbow is: lots of colors, but still one rainbow.

Thanksgiving is like a primary color in a rainbow that blends into praise. Then the praise color shines out, strong and clear, and that blends into worship, and the worship color shines out. But all three are essentially one thing — a glorious rainbow of adoration that takes us into the presence of God. It starts with thanksgiving, goes into praise, then culminates in worship.

Start With Thanksgiving

Thanksgiving is what you do when you thank God for what He's done in the past. Do you remember when you were saved? Do you remember when you were healed at one time or another? Do you remember when you were filled with the Holy Spirit? Now when you start thanking God for what He's done — for the time He touched your child or the time He met your financial need when you had to have a miracle — when you thank God for what He's done in the past, that is thanksgiving.

Move Into Praise

Praise is very different from thanksgiving. *Praise is related to God's character and who God is.* God is omnipotent; He has all power. When you start praising God because He's powerful, you've moved from thanksgiving to praise. You can praise God for His love, you can praise God for His grace, you can praise God that He knows all things, you can praise Him for His mercy, for His longsuffering, for His unchangeableness. That is praise, not thanksgiving. Thanksgiving is thanking Him for what He's done, while praise is acknowledging and praising Him for what He's like and who He is. It is directly related to God's character.

Worship in Spirit

Now worship is something different again. Worship is not understood by most believers. Churches call their Sunday morning service a "Sunday Morning Worship Service." Yet very seldom does worship happen in a church on Sunday mornings, because most of us don't know what worship is. Most services are conducted in the realm of thanksgiving, some may get into praise, but very few people ever get into worship. It is not really a worship service until you have walked into the presence of the *Shekinah*, the glory of God.

Worship is directly related to the holiness of God. In thanksgiving, you thank Him for what He's done. In praise, you praise Him for who He is. But worship is what happens to you when you get into His presence, when you sense His holiness.

There is something so very important to be learned about these distinctions. I can lead you in thanksgiving. I can lead you in praise, but I can't lead you in worship. Worship is a result of the sovereign invitation of the Holy Spirit to come inside the veil and to be where God is. Now let me tell you, those are awesome moments. And that is the passion of God's heart for you and me. God wants us in worship. That is where we should be. That's what is in the heart of God. And, friend, whether you know it or not, that's the passion and the desire and the hunger inside of you — to be where God is. It's a powerful drawing force that few believers understand.

Walking Through the Tabernacle of Moses

We have seen how thanksgiving starts us moving from where we are toward the presence of God. It takes us into the outer court of the Tabernacle. But our desire is not to remain there, but to press on until we come into the Holy of Holies, into the very presence of God.

Inside the Tabernacle of Moses, there were seven pieces of furniture. Two were in the outer court. The first one was a brass altar. The second one was a brass bowl of water that the Bible calls a laver.

Once you walked inside the tent, into the Holy Place, over on your right you would see a table and twelve loaves of bread on top of the table. That was called the table of show-bread. Immediately across from this, on the other side of the Holy Place, was a seven-branch golden candlestick with bowls of oil set afire which gave light to this area of the Tabernacle. Then immediately in front of the veil was a golden altar of incense. That was the fifth item of furniture in the Tabernacle.

Behind the veil, in the Holy of Holies, were the last two items of furniture. First, there was the Ark of the Covenant. The ark was a chest or a box that contained Aaron's rod that budded, the manna that God sent to feed the children of Israel after they came out of Egypt, and the tables of the Ten Commandments that Moses brought down from Mt. Sinai. These three things were inside the Ark.

The mercy seat was on top of the Ark. It was on the mercy seat that the high priest put the blood of the lamb. When the blood was put on the mercy seat, the sins of the entire nation were covered for a year. *The presence of God, the Shekinah, dwelt between the cherubim immediately over the mercy seat.*

Whenever the high priest went from the outer court, through the Holy Place, and into the Holy of Holies, to the mercy seat, he had to stop at every station along the way. And that's the same pattern the Holy Spirit has given to us so we, too, can come into the presence of God.

In the outer court, you stop at the brass altar, which stands for the blood of Jesus. You come to the brazen laver, which stands for God's Word. When you walk into the Holy Place, which represents the soul of man, you stop at the table of showbread, which is the soul of man, and you deal with your will. You come to the golden candlestick, and you deal with you mind. You come to the golden altar of incense, and you submit your emotions. You move through the veil, into the Holy of Holies, and you come to the Ark of the Covenant, where sin is covered. And you come ultimately to the mercy seat where the presence of God is manifested, and you are with the Father and the Father is with you.

The Holy Spirit has given us a powerful picture in this. I practice these steps regularly. I kneel by my bed, or wherever it is that I make my time to be with God, and I simply walk through the Tabernacle of God. This is not difficult or theological, yet it is absolutely infallible — if you will follow the steps given to us in the pattern of the Tabernacle furniture, you will get a sense of the presence and the power of God. You will come right into His very presence in the Holy of Holies.

2

Overcoming Guilt
The Brazen Altar

GOD IS A HOLY GOD. He loves us and wants to fellowship with us, but cannot, because we are sinners and He is holy. His holiness will not allow it. Yet His desire for our fellowship was so great He made a creative plan. He would make us like himself so we could come into fellowship. He would make us righteous. He solved the problem of our sin and guilt.

IN THE DAYS OF MOSES, when a Hebrew wanted to seek after God, he would leave his little tent out in the encampment, select his sacrificial animal, and bring it to the Tabernacle, situated in the geometric center of the camp. From afar off, he could see the great fence of white linen around the outer court of the Tabernacle. As he approached the dazzling white curtain of the imposing structure, his heart would be filled with awe and reverence for the God who had brought him out of bondage in Egypt with signs and miracles.

As the Hebrew man walked through the entrance with his animal, there before him would be the altar of brass, or the brazen altar. It was seven-and-a-half-feet square and four-and-a-half-feet tall. It was made of acacia wood and covered with brass, polished so brightly you could see yourself in it. It was the largest piece of furniture in the entire Tabernacle, and it completely dominated the entrance. A priest would be waiting at the brazen altar to meet the man and assist him in the sacrifice.

There is an important pattern here for New Testament believers. You could not get into the presence of God without stopping at the brazen altar, the place of sacrifice and shedding of blood. Here is where you found forgiveness for sin. The brass altar was the first thing seen; it was the piece of tabernacle furniture that was used most.

The Four Aspects of Forgiveness

On the altar there were four horns. When an animal was put on the altar to be sacrificed, it was tied on the horns of the altar. The four sides of the altar have a particular significance for us, because as each person came to seek God, four steps were taken at the altar of brass, revealing four aspects of divine grace and God's love.

Step One: Confession of Sins

When a person came to this altar, he wanted to have peace with God. The first thing to do to have peace with God was to have his sins forgiven, so he would confess his sins and ask God to forgive him. That's the first action to be taken when one comes to God.

If you're going to get into the presence of God in your own devotions, the first thing to do, as you start your prayer time, on your way into the presence of God, is to start it with an action of experiencing the forgiving power of God. If you've made mistakes, whatever they may have been, ask for forgiveness so you can receive the forgiveness of the Lord.

You know, it's a hard thing for a man to receive God's forgiveness. Most people feel like they've got to *earn* forgiveness one way or another. Most religions of the world are composed of people who are trying to earn God's forgiveness by good works, by gifts, by religious activities, or by punishing their bodies; all these people are doing *something* to try to earn the grace and the mercy of God on their own.

But you can't come that way. When you come to God for forgiveness, you must come in His way. You must come with a sacrifice.

Step Two: The Sacrifice Is Made

After a person confessed his sins, an animal was slain at the altar. Some people don't like a religion that has blood in it, but you cannot understand the grace of God until you are willing to look at the shedding of blood. A man who went into the Tabernacle of Moses did so not only to have his sins forgiven, but also to have his sin put away, to have it covered, to have it cleansed.

The Hebrew man would bring an animal, most often a lamb, with him for a sacrifice. He would come to the altar and meet the priest. Then he would lay his hands on the head of the lamb, and he would confess his sins before God, imputing his sin to the lamb so that the lamb became guilty in his place, for his sin. So when the lamb was slain for his sin, he was freed of his sin because his sin had been transferred to the lamb.

This is what happened at Calvary when Jesus became sin for you. Do you remember what John the Baptist said when he saw Jesus coming? He said, "Behold the Lamb of God." Jesus was the Lamb of God. Jesus was the sacrificial animal that was slain. Your personal sin killed Jesus Christ. Never forget that. The altar was not a brass altar; the altar was the cross. When Jesus died on the cross, He fulfilled this symbolism and this pattern. So in Jesus Christ we have remission of sins; our sins are blotted out forever.

Second Corinthians 5:21 says that God *"made him* [Jesus] *who had no sin to be sin for us, so that in him we might become the righteousness of God"* (NIV). Jesus Christ received your sin. He was the sacrificial lamb. It was God in heaven who put your sin upon Jesus, much like the man would lay his hands on the head of the lamb and confess his sins over the lamb. God did that to Jesus on the cross. And Jesus became filled with your sin. God made Him who had no sin to be sin for us. It was your sin that killed Jesus. Until you see that, you can never know the power of redemption in your own life.

You see, sin has to be paid for. You can't just push sin over in the corner and pretend God doesn't see it. Every sin that every man has ever committed has to be paid for. And Jesus paid for them all.

I once heard a famous evangelist tell a story that I have never forgotten. He was traveling in the southern United States, and he was late for a meeting. He was driving a car and he was speeding! He was pulled over by a local policeman. Immediately when the policeman realized who he'd stopped, he said, "We take care of our traffic tickets immediately in this county. I'm taking you in to the justice of the peace, and we're going to see what the judge says." So he took the well-known minister in.

The justice of the peace in that county was also the local barber. So they brought the evangelist into the local barber shop and held a session of court.

The barber recognized him immediately when he came in. He said, "What are *you* doing here? Driving too fast, I understand?"

The man of God hung his head and said, "Yes, I was driving too fast. I was speeding."

The official responded, "Well, you're guilty, aren't you?"

"Yes, I'm guilty."

"All right, that will be thirty dollars in costs," the judge said. "When the law is broken, a penalty must be paid. I cannot let you off, because I am an officer of this court. If I let you go that would be unfair."

The evangelist reached into his wallet to pull out the money, but the judge said, "No, just a minute. I've been a real follower of your ministry for years and you have been a blessing to me and my family. I'm going to pay the fine for you." The judge then took the money out of his own pocket, and put it in the cash register to pay for the ticket. Then he said, "You, sir, are free to go."

You see, the evangelist couldn't just say, "I'm sorry," and let that be the end of it. The crime had been committed and someone had to pay. But, as this story shows, somebody other than the guilty party can pay for their mistake.

And that's what Jesus did for you. *Jesus paid the price for your sin.*

In the Tabernacle of Moses, the Hebrew man prayed and confessed his sins over the head of the lamb, then the priest cut the throat of the lamb and gathered the blood in a basin. Of course, the animal died instantly. Then the priest would take a small amount of that blood, and he would sprinkle it on the man who brought the sacrificial animal. He would then speak over him and absolve him of his sin and guilt.

The whole principle to be understood here is that innocent life has been given for sin. Everyone in ancient Israel realized that their sin had been covered or cleansed by the death of an innocent animal. In our day, we need to realize that our sin can only be covered and cleansed by the death, not of an innocent animal, but of the Son of God. Jesus Christ died and paid the price for your sin. If you accept Him as your Savior, then you know this, and you have an assurance in your heart that your sin is covered by the blood of Jesus Christ. Praise God!

Perhaps you would like to accept Jesus as your Savior now. If so, pray this prayer, saying:

Jesus, I believe that you are the Son of God. I believe that you came to the earth to pay for my sins. I believe that you died, and rose again, and that you are alive today. Jesus, I ask you to forgive my sins, and make me a part of your wonderful family. I ask you to come and live inside of me, and be my Lord. Amen.

Step Three: The Burning of the Sacrifice

The third thing that happened at the altar of brass was that the sacrifice was placed on the altar and then burnt. This symbolically represents the Crucifixion of Jesus Christ on the cross. The Bible says (in Romans 6:6) that our "old man," that rebel nature inside of us, that part of us that wants to sin, was crucified with Christ on the cross. We have died to sin; we've died to the flesh.

We are referring here, not to sins, but to sin itself. There is a difference between sin and sins. Sin is the factory; sins are the product of the factory. You could ask God to forgive you for doing this, that, and the other thing, but you would still be a sinner. The sin factory is still at work, causing you to sin.

But, praise God, there is a double work in Jesus Christ. There is a way to get rid of the sin principle. The answer for your flesh, and that old nature, is not education, or pampering, or anything like that. The only thing that is good for your flesh is crucifixion.

That is what happened at the brazen altar: the flesh of the sacrificial animal was burned. And that's what happened with Jesus Christ on the cross. When He died, our flesh was destroyed, and our sin nature was crucified.

Step Four: Consecration for Service

A fourth thing happened at the brazen altar: the priest would consecrate himself for service. You see, the priest could not offer forgiveness and cleansing to anyone else until he had offered a sacrifice for his own sin. Everyone was guilty before God, so even the priest had to offer a sacrifice for himself. The priest would bring his own sacrificial animal to the same altar, take the animal, and shed the blood. Then he would take the blood of the animal and touch himself with it on the right earlobe, on his right thumb, and on the big toe of his right foot.

This symbolized that he was dedicating and consecrating his body as a priest unto God. First of all, he would dedicate his hearing — he would hear the voice of the Lord. Secondly, he would dedicate the work of his hands — his service to God would be cleansed by the blood, sanctified, dedicated, and consecrated to God. Then, by applying the blood to his big toe, he dedicated his pathway, declaring that he would walk in ways that would be pleasing to God.

This is what Paul referred to in Romans 12:1: *"Therefore, I urge you, brothers, in view of God's mercy, to offer your bodies as living sacrifices, holy and pleasing to God – this is your spiritual act of worship"* (NIV). This is a picture of the Hebrew priest coming to the brazen altar and presenting his body as a sacrifice, putting the blood on his right earlobe, his right thumb, and the big toe of his right foot.

By way of this picture, Paul is saying to us, "I beg you, as children of God, by the mercies of God, to present your bodies as living sacrifices, holy and pleasing to God. It is your act of worship, your reasonable service." In verse 2 he goes on, *"Do not conform any longer to the pattern of this world, but be transformed by the renewing of your mind. Then you will be able to test and approve what God's will is – his good, pleasing and perfect will"* (NIV).

This is how we begin our journey into the presence of God. You cannot start your devotions, you cannot start your journey, you cannot start coming into the presence of God until you have first taken care of the sin question in your own life. It's a good thing to know the up-to-date value of the blood of Jesus in your life every day!

We start here at the altar of brass, and we confess our sins. We declare the power of the blood of Jesus to completely remove all trace of sin, and we acknowledge that our sin nature was crucified with Christ. Then we dedicate our-selves as a living sacrifice to God for service.

Solving the Problem of Guilt

Once sin is confessed and removed by the blood of Jesus, in God's eyes, we become pure and righteous, and our sin is no longer a problem. Even so, ninety-five percent of Christians have an incredible problem with their own guilt. Guilt is the biggest problem I know of in the Church, and this is so because the devil knows how to hit your "hot button."

The Accuser of the Brothers

Let me show you how the devil operates. Revelation 12, verses 10-11, records a battle in the heavenlies — the devil has been fighting against the angels of the Lord, and Satan has been cast out of heaven. Verse 10 says: *"Then I heard a loud voice in heaven say: 'Now have come the salvation and the power and the kingdom of our God, and the authority of his Christ. For the accuser of our brothers, who accuses them before our God day and night, has been hurled down'"* (NIV).

Notice what the devil is called — *"the accuser of our brothers."* Not *an* accuser, but *the* accuser of our brothers. If you're a believer in Christ, then you're one of the "brothers," and the devil is your accuser.

The main job of Satan every day of your life is to make you aware of your sin, accusing you, and robbing you of the sense of victory that comes by the finished work of the blood of Jesus.

The devil knows when you've failed, when you've made a mistake, and he knows how to make you feel guilty about it. He knows how to get you out of victory and away from the presence and the awareness of the power of God in your life and to tie you up in knots because you make mistakes and you fail. Satan's job is to accuse you in your marriage and accuse you with your children. He'll accuse you in your finances. He'll accuse you of sin and lust. He'll accuse you of everything he can because that's his business.

For most believers, guilt is the greatest barrier that keeps them from the presence of God. They labor under a load of guilt that leaves them feeling separated from God. Many actually believe that they are being convicted by the Holy Spirit. The devil has used guilt as his tool for centuries in the guise of Holy Spirit conviction. The Holy Spirit calls you to repentance, to turn from sin. Guilt tells you, "You're too weak. You've fallen before and you'll fall again. You just don't have what it takes. Why even try again? You might as well give up."

Can you see how Satan accuses you? He does it by putting his thoughts into your mind. Half of the time when you're thinking, the thoughts are not your thoughts, they are thoughts from the enemy. He fires thoughts into your head — constantly!

In my early walk with God, I didn't believe negative thoughts came from the devil because I couldn't understand *how* he could trigger a thought in my brain. Then one day I realized that Satan has *always* done his business through thoughts. That's what he did to Eve in the Garden of Eden. He said to Eve, *"Hath God said...?"* That's a doubting thought. He made Eve doubt what God said. Sin was born in the human race because Eve listened to the thoughts of the devil.

In the New Testament we read about the betrayal by Judas, *"Now Satan having put into the heart of Judas to betray Christ...."* Jesus Christ was crucified by a thought that the devil had placed in the heart of one of Jesus' closest friends.

And Satan is still doing this. He can use a thought to wreck your marriage. He can even tell you that you ought to divorce your wife. He can tell you that your husband is cheating on you. Just a whisper, just a thought — that is how Satan does his work.

The Power of a Thought

How many of you know that God, on the other hand, leads us by divine thoughts? The problem is, believers hear both sets of thoughts and they wonder which ones come from God and which ones come from the devil. As you continue to walk with God, you start to know whose thoughts you are hearing. Jesus promised you would. He said, "My sheep know my voice." Every day of your life you need to check up on where the thoughts that you're thinking have come from.

God has given me some amazing thoughts at times. Sometimes when I preach, God will tell me about someone in my audience. I was preaching a three-day meeting several years ago in Virginia. During the Sunday night service, the Spirit of God came on me during the altar call, and He revealed startling information about a man in the room. I said, "There is a man in this building who has purchased a gun and he's planning to kill his wife." I went on, "The Holy Ghost is telling me all about you right now, and He is telling me this in order to put you under conviction."

I had never said anything like that in a public meeting in my life. I was surprised as the words came out of my mouth. But I knew it was God. Therefore, with confidence I said, "I'm going to wait here at the end of this service. Whoever you are, I want you to come and talk to me." Well, I promise you, I had everyone's attention at that point. All the ladies were looking at their husbands. When the meeting was done, I stayed at the front. None of the men would come within ten yards of where I was standing. I was the loneliest man in church!

The man did not come forward. In my motel room that night, I asked the Lord about it. He assured me that the man was there and that he had heard what I had to say.

The next morning, the phone in the church office started to ring. The ladies were calling in to ask, "Pastor, did that man give his life to Christ last night?"

The pastor would say, "No, he didn't."

The ladies would say, "You mean, he's still on the loose? What are we going to do?"

He would say, "Well, come back tonight and let's see what happens!"

We had more people in church on Monday night than we had on Sunday night! On Monday night, the power of God came down in the healing service. There was an athlete who had torn all the ligaments in his knee in an athletic injury. The power of God hit his knee, and his knee was instantly healed. He was running around the room, and people were getting healed throughout the sanctuary.

Then from one side of the room I saw a man run to the front and fall on his face. A church worker went over to him and prayed for him, leading him to Jesus. The church worker walked over to me later and said the man who was planning to kill his wife had just given his heart to Jesus. I got excited!

At that time I was on seventeen major radio stations across the nation, and on my radio program, I told about this supernatural event. Three weeks later I received a letter from a man in Phoenix, Arizona. He had purchased a gun and was planning to kill his wife. He had been driving down the freeway at precisely 11:00 in the morning. As he scanned through the stations on his radio, he came to the one that was broadcasting my program. He said it was like God started to talk to him through the radio. He slammed on the brakes, pulled over to the side of the freeway, raised his hands, cried out to God and said, "Lord, forgive me."

He then went home and confessed to his wife, and told her what he had been planning. They got their marriage back together again. They both got right with God, and their marriage was transformed. When he wrote the letter to me, I could hardly read some of the words because there were tear stains on every page. The man had been miraculously transformed by the grace of God.

All God gave me in the meeting that Monday night was a thought. But that thought, acted upon and spoken out, was a powerful force that changed lives.

The devil also knows the power of a thought. He has access to your mind, and can give you thoughts just like God can. Have you ever been praying, talking in the spirit, and fellowshiping with God when an evil thought comes into your mind? Such a thing has happened to everybody. Where did that evil thought come from? The devil accessed the computer of your mind and fired the thought in.

The Trap of Guilt

Guilt is the devil's primary method of attack. He whispers in your ear, "How in the world do you think you're going to continue to serve God when you keep blowing it and falling flat on your face, committing the same sins over and over? How long do you think God is going to keep on forgiving you?"

When guilty thoughts come and make you feel like you're useless and you'll never make it, you can be sure that those thoughts are not from the Holy Ghost. The Holy Ghost doesn't beat you over the head if you're trying to serve God. God will never make you feel guilty and worthless.

No, the devil is trying to trap you with guilt, because when you feel guilty, you can't believe God for miracles, because you feel so unworthy. You have no basis for your faith. You can't pray. You can't be healed. You can't really praise the Lord. You can't believe for finances or miracles. In fact, you can't believe for anything because your guilt has robbed you of your peace with God.

The Bible says, in 1 John 3:21, *"Dear friends, if our hearts do not condemn us, we have confidence before God"* (NIV). But if your heart is condemning you, then you have no confidence before God, and the devil has successfully done his job of accusing you.

Satan is after you every day of your life. He is trying to destroy the power of the blood of Jesus in your life because he wants you to get your eyes off of the power of the blood and on to the power of your own sin and the power of your own mistakes.

Let me tell you, if you've got your eyes on your mistakes, you're going to continue to make them. Some preachers continually tell people to stop sinning: Stop this, and stop that, and stop something else, and all that the people can see is what they're not supposed to do. But in the process of trying to stop sinning, they can't, because they have their eyes on the sin and that's all they can see.

The Hypnotic Power of Sin

My father is retired, but he used to minister in a Pentecostal denomination in Canada. Once he told me a story I've never forgotten. A minister-friend of his had been invited to a zoo by the zookeeper, who was also a believer. They had just imported a new snake from Africa. The zookeeper said to the minister, "Come and look at this snake. It is the most unusual reptile I've ever seen."

The minister came to the snake's cage and watched as the zookeeper took a little sparrow, opened the door of the cage, and threw the sparrow in. The snake was coiled in the corner and didn't move at all. When the sparrow saw the snake, it was terrified. It fluttered way up in the corner of the cage, as far away from the snake as it could get. The snake did nothing, it just fastened its eyes on the bird and began to watch.

The minister was intrigued. He said, "I watched that little bird stop fluttering and become attracted by the eyes of the snake. He literally became hypnotized. The little bird flew down onto the ground and hopped across the floor. The snake opened its mouth, and the little bird jumped in."

He said, "When I saw that, I realized what Paul meant in the Bible when he talked about the mystery of iniquity.

There is a power in sin. There is a power in the eyes of the snake. When you're trying not to do something, you are sure to go back and do it, because you are hypnotized by the thing you're trying to stop. And when you preach law to people, you only bind them into legalism. When you preach grace and the power of God, you get their eyes off of the snake and onto the power of God."

So get your eyes off the snake and get your eyes on the blood of Jesus!

The Answer to Guilt — God's Righteousness

There is only one answer to the accusations of the devil in your heart and life, and that is righteousness — the righteousness of God. Remember, we read in 2 Corinthians 5:21, that God made Jesus to be sin for us who knew no sin that we might be made the righteousness of God in Him. I call that verse the *divine exchange.* When you trusted Christ as your Savior, God took your sin, all of it, and He put it on Christ. And then He took the righteousness, the absolute pure beautiful righteousness of Jesus, and put it on you. God made Him sin with your sin and made you righteous with His righteousness.

There is no such thing as being two-thirds righteous. Your righteousness is not based on the fact that you read your Bible this morning, or that you witnessed to somebody, or that you paid your tithes. Your righteousness has nothing to do with what you've done. Your righteousness is a gift of God. He took the righteousness of Jesus and He conferred it on everyone who would trust Christ and trust the cleansing of the blood. Then He took your sin and He put it on Jesus.

When we continue to walk in guilt and condemnation, we are actually telling God, "I don't believe in your gift of righteousness. I don't appreciate the tremendous price Jesus paid in taking my sin on himself."

You may look at yourself and say, "But I make mistakes." That doesn't matter. In the eyes of God, because you are cleansed by the blood, you are righteous.

God does not grade on a curve. You're either 100 percent righteous or you're not even a believer. You've got to make up your mind, what are you? There is no such thing as half-righteousness. You either are righteous or you are not.

Don't let the devil talk you out of your righteousness! When we make a mistake, and blow it, the devil is quick to remind us. He wants us to think, "How can I be righteous? I made a mistake." God is aware that we all make mistakes. He gave us the blood of Jesus to continually cleanse us from sin, but we've got to walk in the power of that cleansing.

Tell the devil, "Satan, you're a liar. I am righteous." You can say that because the Word of God says it, and if God's Word says it, then you say it. When you line your mouth up with God's Word, you are lining yourself up with the power of God.

Let's read Revelation 12, verses 10 and 11, again:

Then I heard a loud voice in heaven say: "Now have come the salvation and the power and the kingdom of our God, and the authority of his Christ. For the accuser of our brothers, who accuses them before our God day and night, has been hurled down. They overcame him by the

blood of the Lamb and by the word of their testimony." (NIV)

You are to overcome the accuser by the blood of the Lamb and by the word of your testimony. But what does that mean? The devil is going to attack you every day with accusations. He tries to make you feel bad, guilty, and negative. He tells you that you're failing all the time. There is only one way to deal with those thoughts, and it is by the blood of the Lamb and the word of your testimony.

Here is what I believe the Bible teaches. You've got to say with your mouth what the Word says. This is your testimony. You say what the blood of Jesus does for you.

You say, "According to 2 Corinthians 5:21, I am made the righteousness of God in Jesus. I am righteous because of the blood of Jesus." When you say that with your mouth, you overcome the devil. You cast him down, his power is broken in your life, and you walk in victory every day that you live.

I do this every day of my life. When the devil brings his evil thoughts and accusations and says I'm a failure and I'll never make it, I say, "Listen, devil, I am righteous by the blood of Jesus." When I do that, my faith is ignited. My mouth is giving testimony to the power of the blood. This is a great key to walking in victory with God.

The Undefiled Blood of Jesus

This may be a shocking illustration, but I'm going to give you a lesson in biology. In a natural birth, the blood type of the new child is determined instantly at the moment of conception. Neither the male sperm nor the female egg has any blood in itself, but carries genetic information that will determine what kind of blood the baby will have. The blood is formed by that mystical union, and life is created instantly.

The child is protected by the placenta of the mother from any flow of the mother's blood into its body. The baby is fed by the mother's blood, but never comes into direct contact with the mother's blood. The food from the blood is fed to the child through a filtering system that the Lord has built into the mother's body. A baby can have a different blood type than its mother, because it never comes into direct contact with the mother's blood.

Now let me ask you a question: What was the blood type of Jesus Christ? When the angel came to Mary, he said, *"The Holy Spirit will come upon you, and the power of the Most High will overshadow you. So the holy one to be born will be called the Son of God"* (Luke 1:35, NIV).

The blood type of Jesus Christ is the blood type of the Father. Jesus had a different blood type than His mother had; the blood of Mary was tainted with sin. But the blood of Jesus is pure; it is undefiled, it has power. It has the energy of God in it.

Jesus Christ was slain 2,000 years ago, but His blood is as fresh and powerful today as it was when He died on the cross. The Bible tells us in Hebrews 9:12, *"Neither by the blood of goats and calves, but by his own blood he entered in once into the holy place, having obtained eternal redemption for us."*

Jesus has gone into the presence of God. He is seated at the right hand of the throne of God. The right hand of the throne of God is the mercy seat. Jesus is there for you, and He brought something with Him — not the blood of goats and calves, but He brought His own blood to heaven.

The blood of Jesus is in heaven, as freshly slain today as when He died on the cross 2,000 years ago.

And when God sees the blood that is on the altar before His throne in heaven, He cannot see your sin because your sin is cleansed by that blood. God looks at you through the blood of Jesus, and He sees someone who looks just like His Son. He sees you in the righteousness of His only begotten Son. Hallelujah!

Now, here is the question: How do we get that blood to our address? That blood is in heaven. How do I get it to where I am, to where I am living today? We are taught how this happens in a beautiful story in the Old Testament. Remember when Moses was trying to get Israel out of the land of Egypt, and he performed ten plagues before Pharaoh, the King of Egypt? The tenth plague was an announcement that Moses made to Pharaoh. He said, "The death angel is coming through the land tonight, and the eldest child of every family will be slain by the death angel. It will be a sign to you that God is saying, 'Let my people go. Let them leave Egypt and go back to the Promised Land of Canaan.'"

God said to Moses, "The death angel is coming tonight, but the children of Israel will be protected if they will do exactly as I tell you. They must take an innocent, spotless lamb, cut its throat, collect the blood in a basin, and then sprinkle the blood on the doorposts and the lintel of the house. When the death angel comes through, if he sees the blood on the door, he will not touch anybody in that house, and the eldest son in the family will be saved."

Every family of Israel obeyed. They killed the sacrificial lamb, and gathered the blood in the basin. But how could they get the blood from the basin to the doorpost?

God said to Moses, "Take a weed, a Middle-Eastern weed called a hyssop. Dip the weed in the blood and then sprinkle that blood on the doorpost and on the lintel, and when I see the blood, I will pass over you." So they dipped the hyssop in the blood and sprinkled it. That's how they got the blood to their address.

That is an Old Testament story that illustrates this New Testament principle. How do you get the blood to your address? You overcome the devil by the blood of the Lamb and the word of your testimony. When you use your mouth to testify to what the Word says about the blood, you're taking the hyssop and you're sprinkling it around the doorposts of your life. When you do it daily, the devil can come at you with his accusing thoughts, but those thoughts can't control you and rule over you because your life and your household are covered by the blood of Jesus. You are walking in the power of the blood of Jesus. Hallelujah!

Declare What the Blood Has Done

Now, this is something that I do regularly in my life. On my way into the presence of God, I stop at the brass altar, and I make my testimonies concerning the blood of Jesus. With my lips, I speak the things the Word of God says the blood of Jesus does for me. I speak them to the devil.

What does the Word of God say that the blood does for us? Let's examine some Scriptures:

In whom [*Jesus*] we have redemption through his blood, the forgiveness of sins, according to the riches of his grace.

(Eph. 1:7)

The blood of Jesus does two things for you as this verse points out — it redeems you, and it forgives you. Now, "redemption" is a word that most people don't understand because it relates to slavery. In the Roman Empire, a slave could be bought and given his status as a free man if a great price was paid. And the price paid for the slave was called "redemption."

Jesus paid the ultimate price for us: He paid the price of His blood. And the blood of Jesus makes you a free man in God's sight, a citizen in the Kingdom of God — and there are no second-class citizens in God's kingdom. No matter the color of your skin, your racial background, your financial situation, every man and woman, boy and girl in God's sight is absolutely equal. That is the teaching of the gospel.

According to this verse, you have redemption. You have something else also: you have the forgiveness of sins. That's *all* your sins — past, present, and future. The blood of Jesus has cleansed you of them all. This is something you've got to tell the devil every day.

The Greek word for "forgiveness" in this text actually means "remission." Forgiveness is offered to believers. Remission is offered to sinners when they are born-again. Remission means that God totally blots out the fact that the sin ever existed. It's erased from God's records.

Our Declarations

On the basis of Ephesians 1:7, I make the following two declarations to the devil:

1. "According to Ephesians 1:7, by the blood of Jesus, I am redeemed, bought back, out of the hand of the devil."

2. "According to Ephesians 1:7, by the blood of Jesus, all my sins are completely forgiven right now. They have been remitted."

The next verse I use is 1 John 1:7: *"If we walk in the light, as he is in the light, we have fellowship one with another, and the blood of Jesus Christ his Son cleanseth us from all sin."* The word *cleanseth* in the Greek is in the ever-present tense — it is going on all the time. The blood of Jesus is on the altar before God in heaven, but it is working in you right now, cleansing you *now*. Here is what I say to the devil:

3. "According to 1 John 1:7, the blood of Jesus Christ, God's Son, cleanses me now, from all my sin."

The next verse is Romans 5:9: *"Much more then, being now justified by his blood, we shall be saved from wrath through him."* The word "justified" in the Greek means to be made righteous. It is the same word that is translated "made righteous" in other verses of Scripture.

We see in this verse that the blood of Jesus makes you righteous. So you can say,

4. "According to Romans 5:9, by the blood of Jesus, I am justified, I am made righteous, just as if I had never sinned."

The next verse is Hebrews 13:12: *"Wherefore Jesus also, that he might sanctify the people with his own blood, suffered without the gate."* This verse tells you that you are sanctified by the blood of Jesus. What does *sanctified* mean? *Sanctified* means to be made a saint, to be made holy, to be separated unto God. So, according to this verse, you are sanctified by the blood of Jesus. So you can say this to the devil:

5. "According to Hebrews 13:12, by the blood of Jesus, I am sanctified, made holy, set apart unto God."

The next verse is 1 Peter 2:24: "...by whose stripes ye were healed." The NIV says, "by his wounds you have been healed." The wounds that Jesus experienced were a part of the crucifixion process. His blood was shed when the stripes and wounds were inflicted. Our healing today was provided 2,000 years ago at the cross by the stripes of Jesus. So you can say this to the devil:

6. "According to 1 Peter 2:24, by His stripes I was healed. If I was healed at the cross, then I am healed now. Sickness and disease, you have no place in me. I am healed by His blood."

The final verse is 1 Corinthians 6:19-20: *"What? know ye not that your body is the temple of the Holy Ghost which is in you, which ye have of God, and ye are not your own? For ye are bought with a price...."* What is the price? Paul doesn't say, but we know the price was the blood of Jesus. So here is what I declare to the devil:

7. "According to 1 Corinthians 6:19-20, my body is the temple of the Holy Ghost, redeemed, forgiven, cleansed, made righteous, sanctified, and healed by the blood of Jesus. Therefore, Satan has no place in me. He has no power over me. I

renounce him. I loose myself from him by the power of the blood of Jesus."

Come to the Altar Daily

The brazen altar gives a picture of God's solution to sin and guilt. Here sin is confessed and the sacrifice is made. Here you learn to let go of your sin and to keep your eyes on the blood of Jesus. You give your testimony concerning what the blood of Jesus has done for you.

As you do this daily, you become more and more aware of the truth that you *are* made righteous with the righteousness of Christ. You *are* able to break free of Satan's bondage, even from those things that have held you captive for five, ten, even fifteen years. Sin and guilt lose their hold on you and you begin to walk in power and victory. Hallelujah! Praise God for what the blood of the Lamb has done!

And you have taken your first step in coming into the presence of God.

3

Removing the Dust of Life
The Brazen Laver

EVEN AFTER OUR SIN AND GUILT have been removed, troubles, cares, and concerns can keep us from having a "clear channel" to really fellowship with our heavenly Father. The brazen laver is God's solution to this problem.

ON OUR WAY INTO THE PRESENCE OF GOD, our second stop is at the brazen laver. The brazen, or brass, laver was the second piece of furniture in the outer court of the Tabernacle. The laver was situated immediately in front of the veil into the second area of the Tabernacle, the Holy Place, where only the priests were allowed to go.

"Laver" is a Middle English word for "wash." The brazen laver is a brass bowl for washing. It is described in Exodus 30:17-18: *"And the Lord spake unto Moses, saying, Thou shalt also make a laver of brass, and his foot also of brass, to wash withal: and thou shalt put it between the tabernacle of the congregation and the altar...."*

Moses had the laver made, following the Lord's instructions. Exodus 38:8 tells us that Bezaleel, the man who built the furniture for the Tabernacle, *made the laver of brass, and the foot of it of brass, of the lookingglasses of the women assembling, which assembled at the door of the tabernacle of the congregation.*

In those days, they didn't have mirrors as we know them, since glass had not yet been invented, so women used shiny brass for mirrors. These were probably the first brass mirrors they had ever owned. Remember, they had been slaves in Egypt for 400 years. But as they left Egypt, the Egyptian women gave them jewels and silver and gold and other precious things, including looking glasses and clothes. It must have been difficult for the women of Israel to give Moses their looking glasses, but they gave them out of the generosity of their own hearts so that the laver could be constructed.

Washing at the Laver

The laver was for the priests to use in order to wash themselves, as Exodus 30:18-21 describes:

And thou shalt put water therein. For Aaron and his sons shall wash their hands and their feet thereat: When they go into the tabernacle of the congregation, they shall wash with water, that they die not; or when they come near to the altar to minister, to burn offering made by fire unto the Lord: So they shall wash their hands and their feet, that they die not: and it shall be a

**statute for ever to them, even to him and to his
seed throughout their generations.**

The laver was filled with pure water. If you looked in
the bowl from above, it became a giant concave mirror, and
you could see your reflection perfectly in the water and the
brass of the bowl.

When the priest came to the bowl, he would look in the
water and inspect himself before going into the presence of
God. Then he would take a small basin that was on the side
and dip the basin into the laver, filling the basin with water.
Then he would take the water and wash himself as God had
commanded him to do.

The Bible said he had to wash his hands and his feet.
That is very significant. He had to wash his hands for
service, and he had to wash his feet to guard his pathway and
keep it pure before the Lord. Notice the warning repeated
twice, *"that they die not."* It was very important for them to
wash if they did not want to die.

The Washing of Water by the Word

The brazen laver represents something vital in the
believer's life today. When you study the Scriptures, you will
see time and time again, the Bible declares itself to be a
cleansing agent.

In Psalms 119:9, David wrote, *"Wherewithal shall a
young man cleanse his way? by taking heed thereto according to
thy word."* Young man, if you want to cleanse your way, get
hold of the Word of God because the Word will cleanse you.

In John 15:3, Jesus, talking to the disciples, says, *"Now
ye are clean through the word which I have spoken unto you."*

There was a cleansing action going on in the hearts of the disciples as Jesus taught them and gave them the Word of God.

In Ephesians 5, Paul writes concerning the work of Jesus for the Church. He tells us that the Church is sanctified and cleansed with the washing of water by the Word. In verses 25-27, we read, *"Husbands, love your wives, even as Christ also loved the church, and gave himself for it; That he might sanctify and cleanse it with the washing of water by the word, That he might present it to himself a glorious church, not having spot, or wrinkle, or any such thing; but that it should be holy and without blemish."* The Word washes and cleanses the Church and makes her a bride that is acceptable for the Son of God.

There are three important parallels between the function of the brazen laver and the action of the Word in a believer's life. First of all, the laver was filled with water for cleansing. Secondly, it was made of brass, which in the Bible is symbolic of judgment. Thirdly, the brass for its construction came from the mirrors of the women of Israel. These three points bring out truths that are important for us to see concerning the role of God's Word in our lives. There is a cleansing character to the Word; there is also a judging character to the Word; and there is a mirroring quality in the Word of God. It cleanses, it judges, and it is a mirror.

Washed by the Blood — Washed by the Word

We stated in the previous chapter that the blood of Jesus cleanses, now we are saying that the Word cleanses as well. Does the blood of Jesus cleanse us in a different way than the Word cleanses us?

Yes, it does. It is vital that you understand the distinction between the power of the blood and the power of the Word. They function differently.

The blood of Jesus cleanses you from inner sin. If you have a problem with the sin of rebellion or the sin of disobedience, you need to repent of it, ask Jesus to forgive you, accept the cleansing of the blood of Jesus, and you will be clean.

The Word, on the other hand, cleanses you from the daily dirtiness of living your life. When you hear someone tell a dirty story, or you hear someone taking the name of Jesus in vain, you're picking up the dirt and the dust of life. You haven't sinned — but you have been defiled.

There comes a time when you just want to wash it all off. You want to get it out of your head and out of your system. At such times, you need the washing of water by the Word. The Word of God will powerfully cleanse away the defilement that comes from living your life.

We need that washing of water by the Word every day. Interestingly, what we read from the Word does not have to deal specifically with the problems we are facing. You may not have to read a verse about swearing because someone has been swearing at work; you can read anywhere in the Word of God and it will refresh you. This is because all Scripture has washing and cleansing properties. It will clean out your mind, and it will clean out your system. It's like washing the dust off.

Remember when Jesus washed the disciples' feet? He refreshed and cleansed them in the same way the Word of God will refresh and clean you. This takes us back to what the priest did at the brass laver: he washed his feet. He washed off the dust of life. He prepared and purified himself so he could enter into presence of God.

Using the pattern given to us in the Tabernacle of Moses for our morning devotions, we first come to the altar of brass and declare the cleansing of the blood of Jesus in our lives. Then we come to the laver of brass, the Word of God, and cleanse our hearts by the washing of water by the Word. The blood cleanses from inner sin, the Word cleanses from outside defilement. When you feel angry, distressed, depressed, or just weary and fatigued in serving, you need to be refreshed. You need to come to the Word because this is where you get the washing you need for your inner man.

Let Jesus clean and refresh you the way He refreshed His disciples: *"Now you are clean through the Word which I have spoken unto you."* We need a good time with the Word of God, letting it wash everything off of us.

Four "R's" From the Word

Most believers are not aware of the many things the Word will do for them. First of all, it gives you rest. There is a peace that comes to you when you study the Word.

It will relax you. It will take away the tension. There is a relaxing quality to the Word.

There is a refreshing quality to the Word. It does something inside of you.

There is also a renewing quality to the Word. Rest, relax, refresh, renew. Sounds great, doesn't it? That is what the Word of God does for each of us.

Hiding the Word in Your Heart

It is so important to meditate upon and memorize the Scriptures. That way, whether you're at your job or working around the house, you can be washing your inner man even if you can't sit down right then, open your Bible, and read. You can meditate on the Scriptures because you've got them memorized. As you work, you can know the power of the Word.

That is also a good reason to sing Psalms. I am so glad the church is singing Psalms again. You know, we used to sing about having a cabin "in glory land, in the sweet by-and-by." We would cry a few tears, but there was no real power in the song. We thought it was anointed because the words rhymed at the end of the verse! We are past that now, and we're going back to singing Psalms. When we sing Psalms, we're singing the Word of God, and the Word is washing us and refreshing us.

Sing Psalms on your way to work, sing them in the kitchen, sing them when you're at school, sing them every-where. Let the Word of God wash you! Its cleansing action is powerful in your life, especially when used on a day-by-day basis.

Notice how, at the brazen laver, the priest had to do the washing. He had to dip the water into the basin and wash himself. And you will have to do it for yourself, too. It doesn't happen by osmosis. It doesn't happen just because someone preaches to you. You've got to take the Word and wash yourself with it. You've got to become a doer of the Word. The Word of God has power, but it only has power if you make up your mind to use it.

The Word of God Will Judge Mankind

The fact that the priest's washbowl was made of brass is significant. In the Bible, brass stands for judgment.

Maybe you have never considered the Word of God as a judge. Many believers have not. Many have said to me, "I thought God was the Judge. How can the Word be the judge? Who is the judge? Is God the Judge, or is the Word the judge?"

It is interesting to study what the Bible teaches on this. In Judges 11:27, the Bible says, *"The Lord the Judge be judge this day...."* In Isaiah 33:22, we read, *"For the Lord is our judge...."* There is no question that in the Word of God, God is the Judge.

A lot of people think of God up in heaven with a big stick waiting for them to get out of line, and as soon as they do, He comes down hard on them. But the Scriptures indicate that God is reluctant to judge mankind. It is something that has to be done, so it will be done, but God takes no pleasure in it.

In John 5:22-23, Jesus said, *"For the Father...hath committed all judgment unto the Son...."* In other words, "The Father has given me authority and power to judge, and so I will be the Judge of all the earth." That is something, isn't it? The Father said, "I don't want to judge, so, Jesus, you be the Judge."

But here's another revelation: the Son is reluctant to judge as well. He tells us in John 12:47: *"And if any man hear my words, and believe not, I judge him not: for I came not to judge the world, but to save the world. He that rejecteth me, and receiveth not my words, hath one that judgeth him: the word that I have spoken, the same shall judge him in the last day.*"

Jesus said, "I'm not going to judge. The Father has told me I can judge, but I'm not going to judge."

There is one standard for judging the lives of mankind, and that is the Word of God. In Revelation 20:11, the Bible speaks of the Great White Throne Judgment. The Bible says the dead, small and great, shall stand before God and when they meet God at the Great White Throne Judgment, they are going to be judged by the Word of God. It will be the divine standard. It is the absolute standard of God.

Do you remember the words of Hebrews 4:12?

For the word of God is living and active. Sharper than any double-edged sword, it penetrates even to dividing soul and spirit, joints and marrow; it judges the thoughts and attitudes of the heart. (NIV)

The Word is a judge over your thoughts and attitudes. It will tell you that certain thoughts, imaginations, and arguments must be cast down. In 2 Corinthians 10:5, we read, *"We demolish arguments and every pretension that sets itself up against the knowledge of God, and we take captive every thought to make it obedient to Christ"* (NIV).

The Word of God Is Under Attack

The Word of God has been under attack since the Garden of Eden. When Satan tempted Eve, he asked her, "Hath God said...?"

Satan attacked the Word of God. One of the devil's global strategies is to keep people everywhere away from the Word of God, away from an understanding of God's standard. He knows the power the Word has. If a man doesn't know God's standard, he will sin. So Satan says to mankind, "God didn't mean what He said. You've misunderstood Him."

The question that Satan asked Eve in the Garden was answered by Jesus in the wilderness. Satan asked three words: "Hath God said...?" Jesus gave the answer in three words: "It is written...." That is God's answer to the devil: "Yes, Satan, it is written." Glory to God! God means every word He says! The Word of God is forever established. It is the absolute standard by which mankind will be judged.

For best results, we should approach the Word of God daily to judge ourselves. The communion Scripture that is read every time we come to the table of the Lord says if we would judge ourselves, we should not be judged. It also says many are weak and sickly among us and many sleep. Why? Because they have not judged their own lives according to the Word of God.

The command of the Scriptures to you and me is that we line our lives up with what the Word of God says. If we don't, we'll become weak and sickly. Many people in the Body of Christ die prematurely because they have not judged themselves according to the Word of God. The Word makes this very clear.

I don't want to walk contrary to the Word of God. If the Word of God tells me something, I want to line up with that Word. I want to do it fast. I want that Word to judge me in an honest way so I can walk before God in purity of heart. I don't want to be weak, I don't want to be sickly, and I don't want to die before my time. So it is important that I judge myself with the Word daily.

The Word of God Is a Mirror

Just like the brass laver, the Word of God also serves as a mirror. In James 1:23-25, the Bible says:

For if any be a hearer of the word, and not a doer, he is like unto a man beholding his natural face in a glass *[or mirror]:* **For he beholdeth himself, and goeth his way, and straightway forgetteth what manner of man he was. But whoso looketh into the perfect law of liberty, and continueth therein, he being not a forgetful hearer, but a doer of the work, this man shall be blessed in his deed.**

This verse is very clear. You can't escape the fact that the Word of God is like a mirror, and if you look into it, you're going to see yourself.

What do you do when you go to the mirror in the morning? You groan when you look at your face. You notice your hair has to be combed. That is what a mirror is for. You come to the mirror to examine yourself. You comb your hair, you straighten your tie, you get ready for the day. Mirrors help you check yourself out. A mirror sends back to you a physical image of what you look like.

God's Word does exactly the same thing. It is a mirror for the inner man. You can see what you really are inside when you look at the mirror of God's Word. That's so important to understand.

Let me tell you something about your Bible. When you are reading your Bible, you're not only reading it, but it is also reading you. It will reveal your uncleanness to you, it will show you iniquity, it will show you sin. All of a sudden, as you're reading, you'll say, "Oh, oh, I've blown it in this area. The Bible says to have patience, and I hollered at that lady driver at the light who turned left when she shouldn't have." This recognition will surface in you, and you'll know immediately, "I blew it!"

The Word of God is a mirror. As you look into it, as you check yourself out, you'll see what's inside of yourself. You'll recognize anger that shouldn't be there. You'll recognize impatience. You'll recognize lust. You'll recognize sin. It will become obvious to you.

You see, eighty percent of God's will for your life is already revealed to you in the Bible. You don't have to pray to God about the eighty percent. You don't have to ask God whether you should lie or not. He's already said you shouldn't lie. You don't have to pray and ask God whether you should rob the bank or not. "Lord, if it be thy will, keep all the police cars away while I go into the bank." Now that is a ridiculous prayer. You know it is God's revealed will not to rob the bank in the first place.

You don't have to pray to God with requests like that. Eighty percent of God's will for you is already revealed to you in the Word. It's the mirror, and it shows you what God's plan is for your life.

Now, after we look in the mirror and see what's there, we've got to do what the Word of God says. It is so important that we are doers of the Word and not hearers only. When we see the sin and get rid of it, we find forgiveness, we find cleansing, and healing, and washing. There is a tremendous action of the Word in revealing the power of God to us.

Seeing Powerful Positives in God's Word

In any mirror, you can see bad things and good things. The mirror of God's Word shows you both negative and positive things from the inside. As the mirror allows you to look into your heart, it will show you the sin, but it also shows you more than the sin. When you look into the mirror of the Word of God, you start seeing the powerful things God has done for you through Jesus Christ. You begin to understand you are made the righteousness of God in Christ. You begin to look at yourself and say, "Hey, I'm wearing a robe of righteousness." You declare the work of the blood of Jesus in your life and you say, "I am righteous."

When I look in the mirror, I look at the Divine Exchange. Jesus took eight bad things so that eight good things could come to anyone who believes in His name.

1. Jesus took our punishment and offers us remission of sins (Eph. 1:7).

2. Jesus took our sicknesses and offers us healing and divine health (1 Pet. 2:24).

3. Jesus took our sin and offers us His righteousness (2 Cor. 5:21).

4. Jesus took our death (spiritual) and offers us His life (Rom. 6:23).

5. Jesus took our poverty and offers us His prosperity and abundance (2 Cor. 8:9).

6. Jesus took our shame and offers us a share of His glory (Heb. 12:2 and Col. 3:4).

7. Jesus took our rejection and offers us acceptance into the family of God (Matt. 27:46 and Rom. 8:15).

8. Jesus took the curse and offers us the blessings (Gal. 3:13-14 and Deut. 28:2-14).

When I look in the mirror of the Word, I see what God has provided for His children. I meditate on the fact that I have remission of sins, healing, righteousness, life, prosperity, glory, acceptance into God's family and all the blessings.

Continue to look into the mirror for the positive. If you don't, you will never know you are righteous, because the first time you sin, the devil will tell you you're not righteous — and you'll believe him. Don't use the mirror just to go after the sin. Sin is there, and the Word will show you. Get rid of sin fast, get cleansed, but then continue to look in the mirror of God's Word to see the positive image God sees in you.

Start seeing righteousness. The Bible says that if any man is in Christ, he is a new creation, old things are passed away, and all things are become new. (See 2 Corinthians 5:17.) Start seeing that reality and say to the devil, "I'm a new man. I'm not the old man. I'm redeemed by the grace of God. I'm cleansed by the blood."

As we keep looking at the positive things in the mirror, that image starts becoming who we are. But we've got to keep looking at it until we become conformed to what the Word of God says about us.

You've got to keep looking in the mirror until you see what God sees. You've got to see yourself through the blood just like God sees you. And when you see yourself in that way, you will have faith of such magnitude that nothing you believe will be impossible. When the mirror becomes the total focus of your life, you will start walking in the power of righteousness like you've never known before.

The Real Word of God

Before we leave the brazen laver, I want to ask you a most important question. In the last twenty-five years of my ministry I have discovered that there is nothing more important than this. It is absolutely vital to your faith. The answer, when fully grasped, will change your life as it has changed mine. Here's the question: "What would you define as being God's Word?"

In John 1:1-2, and verse 14, John writes these words, *"In the beginning was the Word, and the Word was with God, and the Word was God. The same was in the beginning with God....And the Word was made flesh, and dwelt among us."*

If I were to ask you the question, "Do you believe Christ is the Word of God?" the answer would be obvious. Yes, the Apostle John makes it abundantly clear that Jesus is the Word of God.

Here's another question: "Why do we call the Book, the Bible, the Word of God? How can Jesus and the Bible be one and the same? Which one is the real Word of God?"

This is a very important question. In fact, it lies at the heart of what I regard as one of the serious mistakes of the Church today. Most believers have given lip-service to the Word of God over the years, yet many believers don't even know what the term "the Word of God" means. That's the reason why the Word of God is not working in their lives. They are playing church.

Several years ago I discovered the answer to this question — and it changed my ministry. I discovered that Jesus and the Bible are both the Word of God. Jesus Christ is the living Word of God; Scripture is the written Word of God. This may sound so very simple, but I assure you, it is not. It is one of the most profound things the Holy Spirit has ever helped me to see. Jesus Christ is the living Word. The Bible is the written Word, but they are both *logos,* they are one and the same.

If your pastor was to announce that Jesus Christ was to be at your church in person for a healing service next Sunday morning, would you have any doubt in your mind that your needs would be met?

That's easy to answer: If Jesus showed up in person, of course we would expect to receive healing and have all our needs met. Why, then, do most believers doubt when the written Scripture is preached in church, under the anointing, that the written Scripture will meet their needs? You see, we look at Jesus differently than we look at the written Word. And yet, when you examine the Scripture itself, they are both exactly the same.

Think of that for a moment. Jesus Christ and the written Word are the same. They are both permeated with God's life and nature. They are both God revealing himself in essence. They are alike in power. Every bit of power that is in Jesus is also in the written Word of God.

Do you remember in John 6:63, how Jesus said, *"The words that I speak unto you, they are spirit, and they are life"*? The words of Jesus are spirit. In John 4:24, Jesus said, *"God is a Spirit."* God is a Spirit, and the words of Jesus are Spirit.

Once you've seen this truth, you can't pick up your Bible the way you used to any more. Suddenly, you will sense life in the words you read. That life will rise up inside your spirit as you meditate on the Scriptures and that life will begin to heal your flesh. The life in the Word will prosper you. That Word will meet all your needs.

I want you to expect the written Word to do for you what Jesus would do for you if He were standing next to you right now.

Your faith must make the same demand upon the written Scriptures as it would make on Jesus himself. Can you see this? The Bible says, in Hebrews 4:12, *"The word of God is quick* [which is middle English for alive], *and powerful."* The written Word is alive in the same way that Jesus is alive.

On Easter Sunday morning you have no trouble singing, "He lives! He lives! Christ Jesus lives today!" The words you read in your Bible are just as alive as Jesus is. There is a living, pulsating, dynamic, divine energy in God's Word. Simply said, it works!

If you can see that, it will change the expectancy in your heart when you come to the Word of God, the Bible. You're coming to it to receive life, to receive power, to receive the energy of God.

Divine Energy in God's Word

The most powerful illustration of this is found in Luke 1. An angel has come to Mary with a message from God. The angel said, "You're going to bear a child. You've not known a man, but you're going to bear a child. And that child will be called the Son of the Highest."

Mary was a young teenager when the angel told her, "You're going to bear a child. He will be called the Son of the living God." Mary was shocked. She asked the obvious question, "How shall this be, seeing I know not a man?"

The angel's reply is found in Luke 1:37, *"For with God nothing shall be impossible."* The word *nothing* is very significant. The Greek words here literally mean *no rhema.*

There are two separate Greek words that are translated as "the Word of God" in the Scriptures. The first is *logos;* the second is *rhema. Logos* means the entire encapsulated Word from Genesis to Revelation. It is forever settled in heaven. Not one jot or tittle of it shall ever pass away.

Rhema means "a word that is spoken." Have you ever read a portion of Scripture 500 times, but one day, it comes alive to you in a new way? It is anointed by the Holy Spirit, and you see something you haven't seen before. That is the word the angel uses in this verse: the revealed *rhema*, the anointed Word of God.

So the angel actually said, "No word that God speaks shall be impossible." Newer translations have it this way: "No word of God is void of power." We could turn around the double negative and put it in the positive sense: "Every word that God speaks contains the power in itself for its own fulfillment."

In effect, the angel is saying to Mary, "The power to make you pregnant is in the Word (*rhema*) that I just spoke over you." What a powerful statement that is!

Picture this: God is in heaven on His throne. He summons an angel, and says, "Gabriel, come here." Gabriel walks to the throne, and God says, "Here is my word. Take it to Mary."

Gabriel comes out of the heavens and appears in the home of Mary. He tells her, "You are going to bear a child. He will be called the Son of the Highest. The Holy Spirit will overshadow you. That which is conceived in your womb will be called the Son of God."

Then Mary asks, "How?"

The angel answers, "Every word that God speaks contains the power in itself for its own fulfillment."

Mary thinks for a moment, then says, "Oh! You mean the words you are bringing to me from God have the power in them to make me pregnant?"

He says, "Yes."

She says, "I believe you. Be it unto me according to your word." And instantly she was pregnant. Instantly! God's Word was fulfilled.

The faith of Mary was necessary for the birth of Jesus Christ. She had to say, "Be it unto me." She had to agree. She had to say, "Lord, I believe. Let your word work."

If you catch this, you'll see it. The word of God was spoken from heaven, carried by an angel, believed on by a woman, and the spoken word of God became the living Jesus in her womb. The Word came out of eternity into our world. Hallelujah!

The Word is brought from eternity into our world every time the anointed Word of God is preached. When your pastor opens the Bible and preaches the gospel, Mr.

Sinnerman, sitting at the back of the church, is convicted in his heart. What convicts him? The Word of God coming out of the pastor's mouth. When he believes that Word and exercises his faith, the Word spoken comes alive through his faith, and Jesus is born in his heart. It is the Incarnation all over again.

In the same way, you as a believer can experience healing, prosperity, and freedom from worry and fear. When the Word of God comes to you, you must make a decision: "What will I do with God's Word?" When you decide to believe God's Word and release your faith, the healing Word comes alive in your body. You have mixed your faith with the living Word of God.

Some Scriptures to Use for Meditation

There are many Scriptures that I use for personal meditation. Often, I will use these verses to build my prayer life and affirm my faith. The Holy Spirit will show other verses for you to use in your personal devotions and meditation.

As you read through these verses again and again, mix your faith with the Word of God, and see these powerful truths become real in your life.

1. **According to Ephesians 1:17-20, I pray that the God of my Lord Jesus Christ, the Father of glory, may give to me the spirit of wisdom and revelation in the knowledge of Him, the eyes of my understanding being enlightened; that I may know what is the hope of His calling, what are the riches of the glory of His inheritance in the saints, and what is the exceeding greatness of His**

power toward me (for I have believed) according to the working of His mighty power which He worked in Christ when He raised Him from the dead and seated Him at His right hand in the heavenly places.

2. According to Joshua 1:8, this Book of the Law shall not depart from my mouth, but I shall meditate in it day and night, that I may observe to do according to all that is written in it. For then I will make my way prosperous, and then I will have good success.

3. According to 2 Peter 1:3-4, God's divine power has given to me all things that pertain to life and godliness through the knowledge of Him who called me by glory and virtue, by which has been given to me exceedingly great and precious promises, that through these I may be a partaker of the divine nature, having escaped the corruption that is in the world through lust.

4. According to Romans 8:11, since the Spirit of Him who raised Jesus from the dead dwells in me, He who raised Christ from the dead will also give life to my mortal body through His Spirit who dwells in me.

5. According to 1 Peter 2:24, Jesus bore my sins in His own body on the tree, that I, having died to sins, might live for righteousness — by whose stripes I was healed.

6. According to Matthew 8:17, Jesus took my infirmities and bore my sicknesses.

7. According to Isaiah 53:4-6, Jesus has borne my griefs and carried my sorrows; yet I esteemed Him stricken, smitten by God, and afflicted. But He was wounded for my transgressions, He was bruised for my iniquities; the chastisement for my peace was upon Him, and by His stripes I am healed. All we like sheep have gone astray; we have turned, every one, to his own way; and the Lord has laid on Him the iniquity of us all.

8. According to 1 Corinthians 2:12, I have received, not the spirit of the world, but the Spirit who is from God, that I might know the things that have been freely given to me by God.

9. According to Mark 11:24, whatever things I ask when I pray, I believe that I receive them, and I will have them.

10. According to Hebrews 9:14, the blood of Christ, who through the eternal Spirit offered himself without spot to God, shall purge my conscience from dead works to serve the living God.

11. According to Hebrews 10:21 and 23, Jesus is my High Priest over the house of God. I hold fast the confession of my hope without wavering, for He who promised is faithful.

12. According to Proverbs 4:20-22, I give attention to God's Word; I incline my ear to His sayings. I

do not let them depart from my eyes; I keep them in the midst of my heart; for they are life to me (for I have found them) and health to all my flesh.

13. According to Isaiah 55:11, so shall God's Word be that goes forth from His mouth; it shall not return to Him void, but it shall accomplish what He pleases, and it shall prosper in the thing for which He sent it.

14. According to Isaiah 40:29-31, God gives power to the weak, and to those who have no might He increases strength. Even the youths shall faint and be weary, and the young men shall utterly fall. But I will wait on the Lord and I shall renew my strength; I shall mount up with wings like eagles, I shall run and not be weary, I shall walk and not faint.

15. According to Psalms 121:7-8, the Lord shall preserve me from all evil; He shall preserve my soul. The Lord shall preserve my going out and my coming in from this time forth, and even forevermore.

16. According to Isaiah 54:17, no weapon formed against me shall prosper, and every tongue which rises against me in judgment, I shall condemn. This is my heritage as a servant of the Lord, and my righteousness is from God.

17. **According to Psalms 23, the Lord is my shepherd; I shall not want. He makes me to lie down in green pastures; He leads me beside the still waters. He restores my soul; He leads me in the paths of righteousness for His name's sake.**

   Yea, though I walk through the valley of the shadow of death, I will fear no evil; for God is with me; His rod and His staff, they comfort me.

   He prepares a table before me in the presence of my enemies; He anoints my head with oil; my cup runs over. Surely goodness and mercy shall follow me all the days of my life; and I will dwell in the house of the Lord forever.

A Daily Habit

Approach the Word daily, expecting it to cleanse you from the dust of life and refresh you just as Jesus refreshed His disciples. As you keep the Word before you, by meditating, singing, reading or listening, receive it as the living Word of the Most High God. Acknowledge that every word that God speaks contains the power for its own fulfillment.

When you meditate on a verse of the Bible that speaks on healing, realize that the energy of God to heal you is in those words. Expect those words to heal your body and they will! Faith comes by hearing and hearing by the *rhema* of God (Rom. 10:17).

As you receive God's Word, it will not only heal you, it will prosper you, it will change your marriage, it will bless your children, and it will bless your home. It will change your life!

Worries and fears will drop away — as you see the power of God move on your behalf again and again.

And you will find yourself with a clear channel to truly fellowship with God in His presence.

4

Thanksgiving and Praise

Entering the Holy Place

THE DESIRE IN YOUR HEART to fellowship with God — to stand in His presence — has never been stronger. You know you are righteous because of the blood of Jesus. You have refreshed yourself in the Word of God. You are ready to take the next step: you are ready to walk through the veil into the Holy Place. But you wonder, "How do I do it?"

DAVID, THE MAN AFTER GOD'S OWN HEART, instructs us how to move from the outer court into the Holy Place in Psalms 100:4: *"Enter into his gates with thanksgiving, and into his courts with praise."* Moving past thanksgiving, and into praise, we move from the outward area of the body into the area of the soul — into the second area of the Tabernacle.

Remember that the Tabernacle was made up of three parts: the outer court, the Holy Place, and the Holy of Holies. We've compared the three parts of the Tabernacle to the three parts of man: the outer court stands for the body, the Holy Place stands for the soul, and the Holy of Holies stands for the spirit. We have also compared the Tabernacle to the various forms of thanksgiving, praise, and worship. The outer court stands for thanksgiving, the Holy Place stands for praise, and the Holy of Holies stands for worship.

Make a Joyful Noise

David paints a vivid picture of worshipers coming into the presence of God in Psalms 100:1, where he writes, *"Make a joyful noise unto the Lord."* Seven times each year, the Hebrew people would come up to Jerusalem and to the Temple to observe their traditional feast days. They sang as they approached the Holy City, steadily climbing higher and higher. The songs they sang are called the Psalms of Ascent, and are recorded in Psalms 120 to Psalms 134.

It is interesting to look at these Psalms of Ascent, because they reflect the spiritual condition of the people as they prepare themselves to worship God. First of all, in Psalms 120, the people are expressing their problems: *"In my distress I cried unto the Lord, and he heard me."* Just like people today, they have problems and spiritual difficulties. They are battling with sin. They are coming up to the Temple, to the presence of God, for help with their problems.

In Psalms 121, they see their answer coming: *"I will lift up mine eyes unto the hills, from whence cometh my help. My help cometh from the Lord...."* In Psalms 122, they express their desire to be in the presence of God: *"I was glad when they said unto me, Let us go into the house of the Lord."* Psalms 123 says, *"Unto thee lift I up mine eyes, O thou that dwellest in the heavens."* You can see a steady improvement in their outlook as they sing. They are getting their minds off their problems and onto the Lord.

Psalms 133 declares, "*Behold, how good and how pleasant it is for brethren to dwell together in unity! It is like the precious ointment upon the head, that ran down upon the beard, even Aaron's beard: that went down to the skirts of his garments.*" As the people approach Jerusalem, they are singing together and making a joyful noise. This Psalm expresses their unity and singleness of purpose.

When they finally reach the Temple, they are ready and their hearts are prepared. David describes the next step in Psalms 100:4: "*Enter into his gates with thanksgiving, and into his courts with praise.*" Singing together in unity got them to the Holy City, but thanksgiving is what brought them through the gates, into the outer court of God's Temple.

Blueprint for a Worship Service

We have so much to learn, both corporately and individually, about entering into the presence of God in a worship service. The clear, biblical pattern is given here: don't start with praise, don't start with worship—*start with thanksgiving.*

This is a mistake often made by pastors and music directors: they are not sensitive to the spiritual condition of their people. If the pastor has been in prayer before the service, he may be in a contemplative mood. He is ready to worship, so he stands up and leads the congregation in a slow worship chorus.

But for the most part, the people are not ready to get right into something solemn when they walk through the front doors of the church. The businessmen have been dealing with the affairs of life, trying to scrape together enough money to get the bills paid. The ladies have been getting the kids ready and out the door in time. Everyone has been all tied up with the hustle and bustle of life. They need a time of transition to move from the outward activities of their lives into the presence of God.

Thanksgiving provides the transition. People come to church thinking about their problems. When they enter into thanksgiving, they start to remember all that God has done for them, how He has delivered them again and again. It builds their faith.

Get Every Body Involved!

The outer court of the Tabernacle corresponds to the human body. In like manner, the first stage of worship should involve our bodies, help us unhook from the hurry of our daily lives, and get us moving toward God. In the outer court, we present our bodies as a living sacrifice, submitting ourselves to the Lord as instruments of worship.

Thus choruses of thanksgiving often involve the human body. You clap your hands with the music or you raise your hands in praise to the Lord. If you believe in dancing, you can use your feet to give thanks unto the Lord. Please, don't put somebody down if they dance before the Lord, and don't put somebody down if they don't dance before the Lord. Let's just be free before the Lord to do what we feel is helpful in bringing our bodies into subjection as we come into the presence of the King of kings and the Lord of lords with thanksgiving.

Songs of Testimony

Songs of thanksgiving are primarily songs of testimony. It is good for us to remember the day we were saved and the emotions we felt when the load was lifted off our shoulders.

Suddenly, we knew that we knew that we knew we were right with God.

It is good to remember when He baptized you in the Holy Spirit, to remember when He healed your body, to remember when He raised your child off the bed of sickness. Go back to the past when you couldn't pay the bills and God ministered to you supernaturally. Somehow the money came in time and made it possible for you to make ends meet.

God has been supplying your needs for years and years. The most important thing you can do in coming into His presence is to thank Him for what He's done.

Giving Thanks Builds Your Faith

An interesting thing happens when you offer thanksgiving to the Lord: your faith grows stronger. God designed it that way. The more you thank God for the way He's helped you in the past, the easier it is to believe that He will help you this time, too.

Did you ever notice what Paul said in Philippians 4:6? He said, *"Be careful for nothing; but in every thing by prayer and supplication with thanksgiving let your requests be made known unto God."*

He said not to worry, but to ask God for what we need. But what must we do first? *"In every thing by prayer and supplication with thanksgiving...."* Come with thanksgiving first. In other words, when you come to God, start with your thanksgiving list, not your shopping list. Don't come to God and say, "God, give me this," and "God, give me that." Instead, come and say, "Thank you, God, you've given me this," and "Thank you, God, you've done this for me."

If you'll focus on the thanksgiving, your faith will be stronger, and it will be much easier to receive the requests you have and the supplications that are on your heart. So come with your thanksgiving list first!

Turning Fear to Faith

One of the most powerful stories of thanksgiving in the Old Testament is found in 2 Chronicles 20. Jehoshaphat, King of Israel, was a godly king who sought after the Lord. But one day, as he was sitting on his throne in Jerusalem, a messenger came from the frontier area and said, "Jehoshaphat, we've just been invaded by three armies. The Ammonites, the Moabites, and the inhabitants of Mount Seir have gathered together and they have invaded the land."

I don't know any word that strikes fear into the human heart like the word *"invasion."* Some of you remember when President Roosevelt announced on the radio, on December 7, 1941, that the Japanese had attacked Pearl Harbor. I have heard Polish people talk about the fear that struck their hearts on September 1, 1939, when the Nazis, under Adolph Hitler, invaded Poland. Suddenly, World War II was underway.

Invasion is a word that strikes fear into the hearts of people everywhere. When a doctor tells someone they've got cancer, they feel invaded. Their body is sick. Fear grips their heart.

What do you do at such moments? How do you turn your fear into faith? This is a fundamental principle that the Church must learn. If I am attacked, if I am invaded, how do I take my fear and turn it into faith?

The Bible says, in 2 Chronicles 20:3, *"And Jehoshaphat feared...."* I like the Bible; it doesn't whitewash or varnish the facts. It tells us exactly what happened. It is very honest. It says Jehoshaphat was scared. He was afraid. He feared. But notice that he took action.

First, he set himself to seek the Lord. That's the important thing. He proclaimed a fast throughout all Judah. Understand, it is absolutely scriptural for a pastor to call a congregation to fasting. There are times when a congregation should come before the Lord and fast for the spiritual welfare of the body.

As the people came together in a time of fasting and prayer, Jehoshaphat stood in the midst of the people to pray. Notice the progression of his prayer.

In verse 6 he says, *"O Lord God of our fathers, art not thou God in heaven? and rulest not thou over all the kingdoms of the heathen? and in thine hand is there not power and might, so that none is able to withstand thee?"* Notice what he is doing — he is ascribing power and glory to God. This is an action of thanksgiving.

Then, in verse 7, he says, *"Art not thou our God, who didst drive out the inhabitants of this land before thy people Israel, and gavest it to the seed of Abraham thy friend for ever?"* In his prayer, Jehoshaphat is recounting what God has done for Israel in the past. He is coming to God to change his fear into faith.

He takes a step toward God in saying, "God, you delivered us in the past. You've blessed and helped Israel in the past. You've given this land to Abraham, your friend, forever. Now what are you going to do in the present?"

The Lord spoke to Jehoshaphat, *"The battle is not yours, but God's"* (2 Chron. 20:15). The following day, Jehoshaphat went out to the battlefield, with his singers marching in front of his fighting men. When they reached the battlefield, they discovered that their enemies were already dead. They had ambushed each other!

Giving thanks is one of the most powerful ways to build faith in your spirit. You may be afraid of bill collectors. You may be afraid of lawyers. You may be afraid of losing your husband or your wife. Whatever it is, if there is fear in your heart, you've been invaded. What do you do? Begin to thank God for all He has done for you in the past. Let thanksgiving turn your fear into faith, and, like Jehoshaphat, receive your miracle!

Two Testimonies of Faith

I live in Tulsa, Oklahoma, and we have two especially well-known evangelists and teachers in Tulsa. One of them is Oral Roberts. As you may know, I am a graduate of Oral Roberts University. I've heard Oral Roberts preach hundreds of times. Many times when he preaches, he tells of collapsing on a basketball gymnasium floor at the age of seventeen. Diagnosed with tuberculosis, he was put in bed and told by the doctors that he didn't have long to live. Then he tells how God supernaturally healed him.

Almost every time he stands up to preach the gospel, he tells that story. *Why?* It is an action of thanksgiving. He is getting his faith ready to bring healing to the people. The way he does it is to give God glory for what He has done in his past.

Kenneth Hagin does the same thing. I've heard him tell his story over and over again. He was sixteen years old and bedfast in the east bedroom of the home in McKinney, Texas. He then tells how God healed him from his terminal illness. Almost every time you hear him teach, he tells the same story. *Why?*

The principle is the same for him as it is for Oral Roberts. In telling their testimonies to an audience, and in thanking God and giving Him glory for what He has done in the past, they are getting their faith ready for what God is going to do now.

That is why I tell my stories of ministry over and over again to a congregation. I don't make any apologies for it, because when I tell a story, it becomes fresh every time. And the faith that comes from me telling that story, not only comes to me, but it also comes to the congregation to whom I'm preaching. It lifts them up and gets them ready for what God wants to do now. Thanksgiving turns fear into faith.

The Sacrifice of Thanksgiving

Do you remember the story in the Old Testament of Jonah, the prophet who was called by God to preach to the people in the land of Nineveh? He didn't like the inhabitants of Nineveh, and he didn't want to go. He tried to run away from God, and got on a ship that was headed in the opposite direction.

A terrible storm arose and the ship was going to the bottom. Jonah finally told the sailors that the storm had come because he was running from God. He said, "Throw me overboard, and the storm will stop." When they threw him overboard, he was immediately swallowed by a great fish.

For three days and three nights, Jonah was in the belly of a great fish. He had seaweed tied around his neck and digestive juices were affecting his body. He was groaning, and he was complaining about his situation, saying, "Lord, everything's gone wrong."

Then all of a sudden, he changed the whole flow of his prayer. In Jonah 2:9 he said, *"But I will sacrifice unto thee with the voice of thanksgiving."* He started to thank God in the belly of a fish. Do you think it was easy to thank God in the fish's belly? No, but that's what he did. He stopped his complaining, and he started giving thanks.

As soon as he started giving thanks, God spoke to the fish. The fish got a stomach ache and immediately deposited Jonah on dry ground. Jonah had hit the hot button: thanksgiving turned his situation around!

I Will Bless the Lord at All Times

I had to learn these principles of thanksgiving and prayer in a very difficult circumstance in my own life. Several years ago, I was awakened about 10:00 or 11:00 o'clock at night in Southern England. The man leaning over my bed had tears in his eyes, and said, "Terry, I have a terrible message for you. Your wife has just been killed in a car accident in Tulsa."

I will never forget that moment for the rest of my life. When I heard it, I didn't believe it. I went into shock. I said, "No, it's not true. I'm going to go back to sleep, and when I wake up, it will all go away." But it didn't go away.

Half an hour later, I was on the telephone telling Misty, Scott, and Rebecca that they would never see their mother again.

On the plane back home to Tulsa, I told the Lord a hundred times, I was done with the ministry. I said, "Lord, this is not fair. After all I have done for you, I deserve better than this."

We had the funeral service in Tulsa. Friends had come from many other parts of the nation, and even other countries. Oral Roberts and others spoke. I made it through the funeral service all right, but when it was done, I went into a spiritual collapse. I was filled with anger, self-pity, resentment, and with hurt. And I kept saying, "God, it's just not fair."

You've got to understand something. I don't teach thanksgiving and praise because I read it in somebody else's book. I've discovered this thing on my own, through very deep trial and pain.

This went on for almost a month. Then Oral Roberts called me one day and said, "I want to talk to you." I went to his office and sat down with him. Three months earlier, Oral and his wife had lost their son, Ronnie, in a tragic incident in Tulsa.

Oral and I read the Word, we cried, and then we prayed. At the end of our discussion, he stood up and he pointed his finger at me and said, "Young man, I am going to tell you something. It will change your life if you will do what I say."

He said, "I want you to go home, get on your knees, and start to pray in the spirit, pray in your prayer language, and start to praise the Lord."

I said, "Oral, I *can't*"

He said, *"You've got to."*

The next morning before daybreak, I was up at 6:00, kneeling by my bed. I was raised in a classical Pentecostal denomination in Canada. I thought we had written the book on praise and worship. I thought I understood what it was. But when I knelt by my bed that morning and said the words, they sounded so hollow.

I said, "Thank you, Jesus."

The devil said, "What for? Your wife is gone."

I said, "Praise the Lord."

The devil said, "What for? You've got three little children without a mother."

For the first time in my life, I had to examine what I meant by thanksgiving and praise. And I found out I was so shallow. I've come to believe that many Charismatics are also shallow in this area, that many of them are simply going through form and ceremony.

But form and ceremony won't help you in a crisis. If you don't have strongly based and strongly rooted praise in your life, you're going to fall flat on your face.

After fifteen minutes of the devil laughing in my ear and saying, "Law, you're a hypocrite," I was ready to quit praying. I was looking into an abyss so deep, I just wanted to chuck the whole thing and feel sorry for myself for the rest of my life.

Then the words of David in Psalms 34 came rising up in my spirit: *"I will bless the Lord at all times: his praise shall continually be in my mouth."* I was like a drowning man going down for the third time and someone had thrown me a life belt. I grabbed onto it and I hung onto it.

Those words were the only hope I had. David said, *"I will bless the Lord at all times."* I said, "God, I may never understand, but I make a decision now. I *will* bless the Lord at all times." And I started to bless the Lord. I said words like: "Hallelujah," "Thank you, Jesus," "Praise the Lord." As I said the words, they sounded so mechanical.

With every word I said, the devil laughed. And he laughed, and he laughed some more.

I was hoping for emotion. I was hoping for some kind of breakthrough inside because I felt nothing and I really didn't know how to handle it. For the first time in my life, I was facing praise that had nothing to do with emotion, and I didn't know how to do it.

I set my jaw, and I said words. "Thank you, Jesus." "Praise the Lord." For half an hour there was nothing. For an hour there was nothing, For an hour and a half there was nothing. For two hours there was nothing.

The devil simply laughed and said, "Law, you're wasting your time. God doesn't even know where you are and He's not interested." After about two and a half hours, I felt something building up inside me like water pushing against a dam. Then there came an explosion in my chest, I never will forget it.

I began to weep and cry and pray. I prayed in the spirit and I prophesied in the spirit. Then I began to interpret back in English what I had been praying in the spirit. It was almost as if I had stepped out of my body. I turned around and I commanded the grief to go. I commanded the anger to get out. I commanded the bitterness to go. I commanded the resentment to be gone.

I don't know how many hours later it was when I got up from my knees, but I knew I was healed. The next day I did the same thing, and the next day, and the next day.

Two months later, the Lord spoke to me in my bedroom and said, *"I've taught you the sacrifice of praise. Now I'm going to send you to my people. And if you'll lead them into my presence with praise, I will heal the sick, deliver the oppressed, and save the lost.*" I've never had a healing service from that day to this when the power of God has not been manifested and the sick have not been healed.

Since that time, God has led a very beautiful young lady into my life. Her name is Shirley. Her husband passed away after two and a half years of suffering with a brain tumor. She watched him slowly die. There was not a thing she could do. She ended up with no food in the house to feed her children. She had to learn the same principles I had to learn: how to praise God in the midst of extreme circumstances.

It Starts in the Outer Court

How do you turn fear into faith? You begin to thank God for what He's done, no matter how badly you feel. It may not be easy; it may take time, you may think your breakthrough is never coming. Just don't give up. I'll guarantee your answer is on its way. You are getting your faith ready for a miracle.

Your miracle starts in the outer court, with your outward actions. I bowed my knee. I submitted my body. I took the words of my mouth, and I spoke them unto the Lord. It was an action of pure obedience because I felt nothing. There was no emotion involved. But in that process, just a little glimmer of faith started to grow in my spirit. And my miracle came. *Praise the Lord!*

When you can't see anything in the present to thank the Lord for, you can always remember when you got saved. You can remember when you got healed. You can remember the goodness of God in your life. You can say, "Lord, I give you thanks for everything you've done." When you do that, you're getting your faith ready. You may not even know it, but something is happening in your spirit.

And when that faith explodes, you're going to walk into the glory and the power and the miracles and the presence of God.

Enter Into His Courts With Praise

In our text, Psalms 100, David declares, *"Enter into his gates with thanksgiving."* Then he says, *"and into his courts with praise."* David is talking about moving out of thanksgiving and into praise. He's talking about moving out of the domain of the body into the area of the soul — about walking through the first veil into the second area of the Tabernacle, the Holy Place.

You will find three pieces of furniture in the Holy Place. These correspond to the three parts of the human soul: the will, the intellect, and the emotions. The will is represented in the Holy Place by the table of showbread. The mind, or the intellect, is represented in the Holy Place by the seven-branched candlestick. The emotions are represented in the Holy Place by the golden altar of incense.

The primary force of the soul is not the mind, nor is it the emotions. The primary force of the soul is the will. There comes a time in your life when you must dictate to your emotions and you must dictate to your mind. You must tell your mind what to do and your emotions what to feel. Your will is the strongest element of your soul, and it plays a very important role when it comes to praising the Lord.

Let's review for a minute the difference between praise and thanksgiving. While thanksgiving involves thanking God for what He has done, praise is uplifting God for who

He is. When you praise God, you look beyond the many good things He has done for you, and you magnify His character and His loving nature which are behind all His actions. You praise Him for His love, mercy, power, grace, longsuffering, lovingkindness, etc.

Thanksgiving and praising God are actions of your will. They have nothing whatsoever to do with the way you feel. If you will learn that fundamental principle, it will change the basis of your praise. You will no longer base your praise on how you feel, but on the fact that God is worthy and you have decided to praise Him. With the Psalmist, you must decide to *"bless the Lord at all times."*

Have you ever noticed where David was when he wrote those words? The little caption that introduces Psalms 34 says that David wrote this when he pretended to be insane before Abimelech, who drove him out, and he went away.

David was running from King Saul. He was being hunted on the mountains like an animal. He went down to the city of Gath for safety. But the King of Gath thought he was a spy and watched him carefully. To fool the king, David acted like a madman, drooling on his beard and scribbling on the wall. His plan worked, and the king dismissed him from his presence.

In the midst of all this, he wrote these words:

I will bless the Lord at all times: his praise shall continually be in my mouth. My soul shall make her boast in the Lord: the humble shall hear thereof, and be glad. O magnify the Lord with me, and let us exalt his name together. I sought

**the Lord, and he heard me, and delivered me
from all my fears.**

(Ps. 34:1-4)

David understood the sacrifice of praise. David understood that praise had nothing to do with the way he felt. He was being hunted. He was nearly imprisoned as a spy. To escape, he was forced to act like a madman. Yet he writes, *"I will bless the Lord."* That is praise.

Real praise is not necessarily what happens in the church meeting where the piano is thundering, and the organ is pumping, and everybody is feeling good. That may be praise, but it is not the *sacrifice* of praise.

The *sacrifice* of praise is when you feel terrible, when you're sick, when you can't pay the bills, when you don't know how you're going to make it. In the midst of the attack of the devil, you make up your mind and say, "I *will* bless the Lord!" It is the most important thing you can ever do. And it's that action that brings you into the presence of God. *Hallelujah!*

Hebrews 13:15 says, *"Let us offer the sacrifice of praise to God continually, that is, the fruit of our lips giving thanks to his name."* A sacrifice is when you give up something to do something else. Most people do not understand sacrifice when it comes to praise. To make a sacrifice of praise, you have to give up doing something else, such as worrying, grumbling, and complaining!

The writer says, *"Let us offer the sacrifice of praise to God continually."* How often is continually? Continually is all the time. You are commanded to praise God all the time. Even when you don't feel like it. That's the sacrifice that's involved with praise.

A Sacrifice Always Costs Us

In 2 Samuel 24, David had sinned by numbering the people contrary to the command of God. He repented before God and asked God to forgive him. The death angel was hovering over Jerusalem, when David repented. God spoke to him, saying, "Make me a sacrifice on the threshing floor of Araunah."

Araunah must have seen the death angel hovering over Jerusalem, for he immediately said, "David, here are my oxen, here are my threshing instruments, here's my threshing floor, you can have everything I've got. It's yours for nothing! Just take it!"

David was faced with a great temptation at this point. He could have made his sacrifice and it wouldn't have cost him a penny. But David had enough spiritual sense to know that sacrifice demands *sacrifice*, and God had said, "Make me a sacrifice."

So David said to Araunah, *"God forbid that I should offer God a sacrifice that cost me nothing."* See, praise that doesn't cost you something is not a sacrifice. It costs to praise God when you hurt: it's that sacrifice that is so acceptable in the sight of the Lord.

Praise in the Midst of the Congregation

We have been exploring the power of thanksgiving and praise in an individual's life. But God has not designed us only to praise Him while we are alone in our rooms. We are also to praise Him, *"in the midst of the congregation"* (Ps. 22:22). In the Book of Acts, tremendous power was released when believers were in one accord: the building shook, the people were all filled with the Holy Ghost, they spoke the word with boldness (Acts 4:24-31); and many signs and wonders were wrought among the people (Acts 5:12, Acts 8:6-8).

Yet, many churches today lack that power. We wonder, "Why don't we see more people get healed?" and "Why don't we see the power of God in operation during praise and worship?"

Shallow Praise — an Empty Ritual

In congregations everywhere, people have learned how to praise God with their mind on auto-pilot. They're going through a form and ceremony. For many, praise is a perfunctory custom, a Pentecostal/Charismatic liturgy. It's something they've gotten into the habit of doing at church.

They put their hands up, they have appropriately pious expressions on their faces, they've got the right words coming out of their mouths, but their hearts and minds are not in it. They're watching what's going on all around them, yet they're acting like they're coming into the presence of God. That is hypocrisy.

How can you walk into the throne room of the King of kings and the Lord of lords, when you're looking all around and your mind is a thousand miles away? These people are not in the presence of God. They're draining and siphoning off the energy and the power of the Holy Spirit that is moving on the rest of the congregation and destroying what God wants to do in that service.

Praise God as an Act of Your Will

In days gone by, when I heard the worship leader say, "Come on, everybody, let's clap our hands and praise the

Lord," I'd just sit there. I'd say to myself, "That guy's not going to hype me. He wants me to be like a little puppet and do everything he's doing, but I don't want to." My spirit was wrong, and my heart was out of sync with God. I didn't understand that I needed to start to praise the Lord before I felt like it.

The Word of God says when you come to the house of God, bring a sacrifice of praise. You need to praise God, raise your hands, raise your voice, and bless the name of God, whether anybody else does it or not. It's an act of your will. It has nothing to do with the way you feel.

The strength of one's will is not well known in Charismatic or Pentecostal circles. Charismatic people are more emotional. If they don't feel the emotions, they won't praise. If the pastor doesn't make a good point, they won't praise. If the choir doesn't sing a good number, they won't praise. Their praise is based on the emotion they feel during the service.

This notion is totally divorced from the understanding of praise as you find it in the Book of Psalms. If you wait until you feel like doing it, you will miss a most vital function of praise in your life. Praise brings you into the presence of God when you need Him the most — when your problems are overwhelming you.

When you come to church on Sunday mornings, it's hard to stop thinking about all your problems and start to praise the Lord. It's easier to just sit and listen to the worship leader's sacrifice, the choir's sacrifice, the soloist's sacrifice, and the pastor's sacrifice, and offer no sacrifice of your own to God. If you do that, no spiritual benefit or spiritual life will flow to you.

Talk to Your Mind

David writes, in Psalms 103, *"Bless the Lord, O my soul: and all that is within me, bless his holy name."* He's talking to his soul. He is moving into the Holy Place. He says, *"Soul, today you're going to bless God."* You've got to talk to your soul when you come into the presence of God.

Tell your mind it's time to praise the Lord. Until your mind has been renewed by the Word of God in a given area, it's still carnal. Paul says in Romans 8:7, *"The carnal mind is enmity against God: for it is not subject to the law of God, neither indeed can be."* So when I bring my mind to church, I've got to tell my mind what to do.

The first thing I tell it is, *"Be quiet!"* You may think I'm being harsh, but I say this to myself: "Mind, you want to think of business, stop it." "Mind, you want to think of problems, no!" Get your mind quiet.

Then start with thanksgiving. Sings songs about the blood of Jesus. Thank God for the righteousness we have through the blood. When a church starts to sing songs of righteousness, and declares their righteousness in the sight of God, it's an action of thanksgiving. They're getting their hearts ready to come into God's presence.

Then start singing the Psalms. Singing the Word washes the dust off and removes the contamination of the world. As the congregation enters into His courts with thanksgiving, their fear is turned into faith. Tremendous faith begins to build in their hearts.

The Holy Spirit may lead you, right then, in the midst of the song service to pray for the sick and you'll see the manifestation of healing. Be sensitive and know when faith is there. Pray for the sick and you'll see the action of God.

Praising God at Midnight

Do you remember the story of Paul and Silas in the Philippian jail? The magistrate had them beaten with the Roman cat-o'-nine-tails, then they were put in solitary confinement in the inner prison. Their bodies ached all over.

Then at midnight, Paul and Silas said to God, "Lord, we would like to retire from the missionary business because it is getting a little too difficult."

Is that what they said? *No!*

"At midnight Paul and Silas prayed, and sang praises unto God: and the prisoners heard them" (Acts 16:25). They weren't singing in a quiet voice. They were singing loud enough so that everyone in the prison could hear them.

Maybe it is midnight for you. Maybe it is dark in your finances, dark in your marriage, dark in your physical body. Perhaps you are dark with loneliness, dark with hurt. At midnight, in the darkness, Paul and Silas began to praise God. Oh, I love that!

And what happened? The ground shook. I heard one preacher say that God loves music, and when He heard those two missionaries singing in the prison, He decided to tap His toe to the music and that's why the ground shook! Someone else said God loves music and when He heard them singing a duet, He decided to make it a trio, and when God sings, He sings bass, and that's why the ground shook! I don't know about those explanations, but I do know one thing — I do know the ground shook!

The next thing they knew, the jailer ran in and said, *"What must I do to be saved?"*

Do you want to get people saved? Teach people thanksgiving and praise and you'll get more people saved than you can handle. Teach them how to praise God in the midst of difficulty. Their fear will be turned into faith, and you'll begin to see God at work in your congregation.

When you do this, when you get everyone flowing in Psalms of thanksgiving, exciting things happen. The people will be getting their eyes off themselves and focused on the glory of God, and you will be on your way into the *Shekinah* presence of the Lord himself!

This is the divine plan of God.

5

The Power of the Will
The Table of Showbread

MANY CHRISTIANS EXPERIENCE a tremendous battle every time they sit down to fellowship with God: their heart longs for the presence of God, yet it seems something always "comes up." God has given each of us a powerful tool to overcome distractions that would keep us from experiencing the joy of His presence: our human wills.

A S WE LEAVE THE OUTER COURT and step through the first veil, we come into the Holy Place, the area of the Tabernacle that represents the soul. As we enter, we see three items of furniture, all made of gold. On the right side is the golden table of showbread, a table with twelve loaves of bread on it. On the left, across from the table, is the seven-branched candlestick, which gave light to this area. Finally, there is the golden altar of incense, immediately in front of the veil.

The three items in this area correspond directly to the three aspects of man's soul: the will is represented by the table of showbread, the intellect by the golden candlestick, and the emotions by the golden altar of incense.

The combination of will, intellect, and emotions make you the unique person you are. They are components of your personality. Some of us seem to have more will power than others, some more intellect, and some more emotional drive. You cannot come into the presence of God until you have dealt with all three.

Your Will Is the Key

There were twelve loaves of bread on the table of showbread, placed in two rows of six. Bread, in the Scriptures, is always a type or a symbol of strength. You get strength from eating bread (Ps. 104:15). I'm convinced that the strength of the human soul is the will.

When God judges mankind on that final day, He won't judge us on how much emotion we demonstrated, or how educated or trained our minds have become. He will judge us on the decisions we have made with our wills.

Your will is the most important part of your soul; the other two parts revolve around it Your intellect and your emotions are to be dictated to by your will, but most of us have the cart before the horse. Many people do not know how to make decisions until their emotions have them fired up. Others don't know how to make decisions until their mind has "all the facts," which makes them susceptible to the thoughts and influence of the enemy.

In approaching the presence of God, your will is the key. You may be made righteous by the blood, and you may be cleansed by the Word, but if you don't bring your will into submission each day of your life, you cannot get into the presence of God. You've got to submit your will to God on a daily basis. You are the one that has to do it: nobody can do it for you.

Jesus, Our Example

Fortunately, we have a wonderful example of how to submit our wills to God in the earthly life of Jesus Christ. Hebrews 10:5-7 gives us helpful insight into a prophecy that was given about Jesus in Psalms 40:

> **Therefore, when Christ came into the world, he said: "Sacrifice and offering you did not desire, but a body you prepared for me; with burnt offerings and sin offerings you were not pleased. Then I said, 'Here I am — it is written about me in the scroll — I have come to do your will, O God.'"** (NIV)

Jesus said, "I have come to the earth to do your will, O God." He came to the earth to manifest the will of God and to submit himself to God's will.

In John 5:30, Jesus said, *"I seek not mine own will, but the will of the Father which hath sent me."* Jesus was able to do powerful works as the Son of God because He did not follow His own will, but submitted His will to the Father. What the Father asked Him to do, He did. That is why He moved in power.

The day before Jesus went to the cross, He knelt in the Garden and prayed. Suddenly, the overwhelming immensity of the task of bearing the sin of the entire world swept over Him. He said to the Father, *"If it be possible, let this cup pass from me: nevertheless not as I will, but as thou wilt"* (Matt. 26:39). He was submitting himself to the will of God.

Friend, this has got to happen in you and me on a daily basis as we come into the presence of God.

In John 4, we find the story of the woman at the well in Samaria. Jesus is sitting on the edge of the well and has asked the Samaritan woman to draw water for Him. His disciples have gone into the city to buy some food. While they're gone, He ministers to the woman.

When the disciples come back they say, "Lord, it's time to eat." Jesus replies with a curious statement: *"I have meat* [or food] *to eat that you know not of"* (John 4:32).

Picture what is taking place here. The disciples have trekked into town, gone to McDonald's, bought a quarterpounder, large fries, and a big Coke. They brought it back to the well and said, "Lord, here's your food. It's all hot, eat it now."

He turns to them and says, "I have food to eat that you know not of." They don't understand Him. The disciples asked one another, "Has somebody brought Him food? Did somebody bring Him food that we don't know about?"

Then Jesus said unto them, *"My meat* [food] *is to do the will of him that sent me, and to finish his work."* Jesus said, "My food, my strength, is to do God's will." Jesus received actual physical strength from ministering to the spiritual needs of that woman. I can tell you, as a preacher, there are many times when I minister to people, when I receive physical strength from God in the process of ministering, because I am being obedient to the will of God.

The Battle in Your Mind

When you set yourself to submit to God's will, you build strength into your soul. You will need that strength, because you face a battle every day that you live — a battle for your will. Satan is a master at getting to your will and affecting your decisions. His tactic? He manipulates your will by influencing your thoughts and your emotions.

We've already discussed the fact that the devil has access to your mind. His negative thoughts can penetrate your mind and exercise great influence over you. He can also cause enough distractions and confusion that it becomes hard for you to hear God's voice.

In the Parable of the Sower, in Matthew 13, when Jesus is describing the seed of the Word falling on various kinds of ground, He says, *"When any one heareth the word of the kingdom, and understandeth it not, then cometh the wicked one, and catcheth away that which was sown in his heart"* (Matt. 13:19).

Let me tell you what goes on during a service when a man of God is preaching. Many of us sit in the congregation and have a battle over concentrating on what the preacher is saying. We are having thoughts about business and thoughts about our children. We can have a thousand different thoughts pressing at our minds, because the enemy of our souls does not want us to listen to the Word of God. Notice these are not evil thoughts, just distracting thoughts. Satan is terrified of what will happen when we hear God's Word, so he comes and catches away that which was sown in our hearts.

The devil is able to influence your thinking, but he can't *make* you think anything. He tempts you by firing wicked thoughts into your head. Then he tries to make you feel guilty for even thinking of such a thing! You are not wicked just because you think a wicked thought, yet that's been his tool in tripping up many Christians for years. He's been firing certain thoughts at you and then you feel guilty for having the thought.

Remember that when this happens, it's not your thought, and you don't have to accept it. Whether you hold on to it or not is your choice. When such a thought comes, you can say, *"Satan, you are putting that thought into my mind. I do not receive it, in Jesus' name. Satan, get it out of here, and get it out now!"*

Wrong Thoughts Make You Sick

Satan also comes after your mind with doubts and fears. He's subtle about this. I recently traveled into a major war zone in Nagorno Karabakh (in Southern U.S.S.R.). I had a life insurance examination before I went. The doctor said, "Tell me, young man, what history is there in your family of heart disease?"

I went down the list. I said, "I had an uncle who died at fifty-two from a heart attack. One of my grandmothers died of a heart attack...." By the time I was done with the list, I was ready for a heart attack myself!

Then the doctor said, "Now, tell me, is there any history of cancer in your family?" As I went down the list, I could sense a knot forming in my stomach. Satan was attacking my mind, trying to get me to receive cancer.

Some believers may have already experienced this. You've said, "Arthritis runs in our family. My mother had it; her father had it. It's been with us for four generations." Your thoughts prepared you to receive it, and you got it because you were ready for it. You spoke it out and put your claim on it.

I am a regent of Oral Roberts University in Tulsa. Several years ago, we had 100,000 people coming through the clinic in the City of Faith every year. I asked Dr.

Winslow at the City of Faith, "What connection is there between thought and disease?"

He said, *"We estimate that sixty-five to seventy percent of disease comes from a psychosomatic origin."* That's about two-thirds of all disease.

In other words, wrong thoughts can make you sick. That doesn't mean the disease isn't real. The disease *becomes* real. There is a real disintegration of tissue; there is real pain. Every part of the disease is there, and a thought started it.

The battle is over your will. Most of the time you decide to get sick. You say, "I think I'm catching the flu." You make up your mind that you're going to get sick, and you speak it out. Because you speak it, you get it. In the same way, you can decide to get well. You can will to be healed by standing on the truth of God's healing Word.

The Battle in Your Emotions

Besides influencing your mind, the devil can attack your emotions, making you afraid. The more you meditate on it, the more your mind gets wrapped up in that fear. Fear is powerful. You can actually sense the flowing of certain chemicals in your body when you are afraid.

At such times, you feel stressed. Your emotions and your intellect are putting pressure on your will, wanting you to make a decision. Most of the time, they are pressuring you to make a wrong decision, or to act prematurely.

The Will Is the Boss

Many people live their lives being manipulated by their thoughts and emotions, and they've never learned the importance of the will. They've never seen the fact that the will is the boss.

You can tell your mind to be quiet. You don't need to receive what the devil's putting into your head. You can tell your mind to throw that thought out and to meditate on the Word of God instead. You can tell your mind what to think, and you can tell your emotions what to feel, because the will is the strongest force in the soul of man. It is in command!

The Table of Showbread

As we enter through the first veil, into the Holy Place, we can see three items of furniture all made of gold.

In Leviticus 24:5-9, we read God's instructions for the showbread in the Holy Place of the Tabernacle:

> **Take fine flour and bake twelve loaves of bread, using two-tenths of an ephah for each loaf. Set them in two rows, six in each row, on the table of pure gold before the Lord. Along each row, put some pure incense as a memorial...an offering made to the Lord by fire. This bread is to be set out before the Lord regularly, Sabbath after Sabbath, on behalf of the Israelites, as a lasting covenant. It belongs to Aaron and his sons, who are to eat it in a holy place, because it is a most holy part of their regular share of the offerings made to the Lord by fire.** (NIV)

The term "showbread" literally means, *"bread of the face."* The presence of God, the face of God, was in the Holy of Holies, separated from this part of the Tabernacle by a veil. It was impossible to stop the presence and power of God from exuding through that veil. The Bible describes the bread on this table as being "before the Lord continually."

God's eyes were on that bread at all times. Your will is what God is after, and He inspects your will twenty-four hours a day. He knows the devil can mess up your thoughts and He knows the devil can mess up your emotions. But He also knows your will is strong enough to rule your soul. *The one thing God wants from you is a decision, an act of your will.*

When Jesus came and preached, the first word He said was, *"Repent."* John the Baptist's message also was, *"Repent."* What does "repent" mean? It means to make a decision. That's the essence of the gospel. The gospel is a message addressed to the will of man.

When you decided to serve God, you made a decision. The devil could not stop you from being born again. If he could have, he would have. But he is not able to go against your human will. Your will is a powerful force in the universe. Each moment of each day, as you decide to serve God, you make the decision, and the devil cannot stop you.

God jealously watches over the will of man to see if he will obey. We're not talking here about obeying God in a negative sense by saying, "Well, I guess I'm going to have to give in to God, because if I don't, He's going to take it out of my hide one way or another."

No, we delight to do the will of God. When you commit yourself to do God's will, you are committing to do the best thing God has for you; and if you'll do His will, God will bless you in ways that are absolutely overwhelming! We delight to do the will of God.

God gave Moses seven points of instructions concerning the showbread. First of all, in making the bread, they were to use finely ground flour. You can't cook good bread if you've got lumps in the flour, so the flour had to be ground. God has a way of grinding our wills, doesn't He? He wants to get out all the lumps! There are times when you sense that God is grinding a little on your will, trying to get you to say, "Yes, I *will* do it. This is the way I am going to go and, Father, *I'm going to submit myself to you.*"

God's next instruction was that the flour be molded into loaves. It was taken by the baker and molded into a proper form. That is what God does to your will and mine on a day-by-day basis. We come to Him in the morning and we submit our wills to Him. We say, "Father, today I am going to serve you. My will is going to be obedient to yours." We are allowing the hands of the Father to take our wills and mold them.

The third thing that happens when you make bread is you bake it. You have ground the flour, you have molded the loaf, and then you put it in the fire. When you make a decision for God, Satan openly attacks, and you come under fire. The fire has a way of burning out the impurities and purifying you.

After the bread was baked, it was to be put on the golden table before the Lord. It had to be put in precise order: two rows, six in a row. Let me tell you something about God. The more I study the Word of God, the more I am impressed with the fact that God is a God of order. When He does something, He does it decently and in order. Now God doesn't say we cannot be open and free and emotional, but He says we should do it *in order.*

If you're going to be like God, then you're going to have an orderly kitchen. If you're going to be like God, then you're going to have an orderly desk. That's the way God is.

God's fifth instruction for the bread was to cover it with frankincense. Frankincense is a spice that, in the Scriptures, always stands for worship. *Our wills are to come to God, not in begrudging obedience, but as worship.* We are to delight ourselves in the Lord, saying, "Thank you, Lord, that I have an opportunity to do your will today."

The final instructions concern the freshness of the bread. It had to be cooked fresh and put on the table every Sabbath day. Then at the end of the week, before the new bread was placed on the table, Aaron and his sons were commanded by God to eat the showbread. Just as the bread was cooked fresh, a fresh submission and dedication of your will to God is necessary every day that you live.

Therefore, Choose Life

In his final address to the entire congregation of Israel in the book of Deuteronomy, Moses gives them one last challenge, encouraging them to walk in God's ways:

> **I call heaven and earth to record this day against you, that I have set before you life and death, blessing and cursing; therefore choose life, that both thou and thy seed may live.**

> (Deut. 30:19)

This is a powerful Scripture, a Scripture that demands a choice. Moses is saying some awesome things here: he's saying that the choice is ours, that it's our decision whether we have life and blessing, or death and cursing.

Make the choice for life and blessing by thinking and speaking about the things that lead to life. If the devil has his way with you, you'll think death and you'll talk death. You'll say, "It's scaring me to death" or "It just tickles me to death." You'll have more ways than one to have death in your vocabulary constantly. You've got to choose life. You've got to choose blessing. You can choose to be blessed. There are ways to do it.

You Have Dominion

When God gave man a will, He made him different from all the other creatures. Man is a free moral agent. Your will is what makes you different. It is the most important facet of your personality and your soul. Nobody can really force you to do anything. Your will makes the final choice. You are the judge, and you make the judgment.

In Genesis 1:26, God said, *"Let us make man in our image, after our likeness, and let them have dominion...."* The first thing God said about man when He made man in His image is, "I'm going to give man dominion." Dominion means the right to rule, the right to make decisions.

The first thing Adam was called on by God to do was to give names to the animals, the beasts, the birds, and the fish. God said, "Adam, whatever you call those animals, birds, or fish, that will be their name from now on and forever." Adam was given dominion. He was given the power of decision.

God created man to rule and not to be a slave. There is no reason to allow the devil to beat up on you every day. God meant for you to rise up and tell the devil to get out of your life. God meant for you to rule in your life, and for Satan to have no control over you whatsoever. That's been God's plan for man from the beginning. The whole decision to rise up and to have dominion is in your will. You decide to stand on God's promises.

Some of you, however, have been beaten up so badly for so long, you don't know how to stir up your will and how to make a decision. You're waiting until you feel like it, or you're waiting until you have every last fact before you make a decision. Making your own decisions is a sacred privilege God has given to you. Don't put it off and let somebody else make up your mind for you.

You may not have God's best in your life. You may be living with second-best because you made bad decisions in the past. If it is possible at all, change the decisions. Make the right decisions. If you'll make the right decisions, you'll be blessed by God.

In the Latin language, I find it interesting that the word for character is a plural noun, a plural form of the singular noun for "habit." In reality, your character is the sum total of your habits. Your habits are formed by repeated decisions. If you make the same decision time and time again, you've got a habit. If you live with that habit long enough, you've got character. If you're going to change your character, you have the power to do it. You have the ability to decide. *God gave it to you.*

Understand one thing: *no decision that you make is unimportant.* You may think, "Well, it doesn't matter. I can get away with a poor choice this time." No, you really can't. Every decision you make has either a positive or a negative effect. It either builds you up or it tears you down. It is vital to watch over your decisions. You have to make decisions for yourself. No one else can make them for you, and God holds you responsible for your decisions.

Forgiveness Is Not a Feeling

One area where making a decision is so vital is in the area of forgiveness. Forgiveness is a decision, not an emotion. Some time ago, while my wife, Shirley, was ministering in another city, she was picked up at the airport by a pretty young woman, very dignified and well-respected in her church. While they were driving to the hotel, the Spirit of the Lord came upon Shirley and she suddenly knew something about this woman—the Holy Spirit told her. She knew that this young lady's father had molested her when she was a teenager.

Shirley revealed what the Holy Spirit had shown her, and the woman dissolved into tears. She told Shirley a terrible story of what her father had done to her, and the hatred and resentment she felt inside for him.

Her life on the outside looked so good. She was wealthy and everything appeared to be going well. But she couldn't forgive her father. For twenty years she had been unable to forgive him.

Shirley talked to her about forgiveness, and she said, "I just can't make myself. I don't feel like I want to forgive him because of what he did to me and how I was degraded by it all."

Shirley had to say to her, "Your forgiveness has *nothing* to do with the way you feel. It is a *decision* that you make."

You may have been hurt by someone very close to you. Maybe you've been hurt in terrible ways. Maybe you are holding an "IOU." They hurt you, so they owe you, because they ruined part of your life.

Many of you have not been able to tear up the IOU's you hold against your husband, your wife, your father, or your mother. They hurt you and you won't let it go. As long as you hold onto it, you think you are paying them back, but really you are destroying yourself. You've got to make up your mind. If they destroyed the first fifteen years of your life, are you going to let them ruin the next fifteen as well by holding onto the IOU?

The Bible says God cannot forgive us until we forgive them! That's the gospel! We pray it in the Lord's prayer: "Forgive us our trespasses as we forgive those who trespass against us." The reason that most believers don't forgive is because they are waiting for a feeling of forgiveness to come. That's a trick of the devil! You don't have to feel anything. You simply make up your mind! You say, *"I will forgive; I will tear up the IOU!"*

When you do it, it is done. It comes out of your spirit, and you decide to forgive. You must make the decision right now. To put it off and say, "I'll think about it later," is wrong. Do it now! Because, if you put it off, you've made a decision not to do anything. Indecision is a decision. When you postpone it, you've made a decision not to do anything. That is just as wrong as saying, "No, I won't forgive."

I have counseled people all over the world. I'll ask, *"Have you forgiven the person who wronged you?"*

They say, "Well, I *love* him."

"That is not what I asked. I need to know, *have you forgiven him?*"

"Well, I *pray* for him."

"But have you *forgiven* him?"

"Well, I knew *he couldn't help it.*"

"Have you *forgiven* him?"

"I really don't *know!*"

Make up your mind to do it. Tear up the IOU's. Forgiveness is a decision. Say this out loud: "Forgiveness is a decision. Forgiveness is an act of my will. I grow strong when I make the right decision."

Repentance Is a Decision

Repentance is another vital decision. Most Pentecostals and Charismatics don't understand that. They think repentance is an emotion, and someone is not really repentant until they are down at the altar, crying buckets of tears: "When you see tears, then you really know they got it because they're crying."

Rubbish! Tears can fool you. Repentance has nothing to do with tears. You can have tears, but they are not necessarily an indication of repentance. *Repentance is a decision.*

Some people are tolerating ungodly habits in their lives. They are messing around with anger. They are tolerating it. They won't deal with their bad temper because they haven't repented. You have to repent before God and get it out of your life. You say, "Well, I can't control it." Yes, you can! It's a decision you must make. Don't blame it on your parents. Don't blame it on your background. Don't blame it on your wife. Don't blame it on somebody else. It is your problem. *Repent!*

You may be allowing other things in your life that are destroying you and tearing away at your life. The only way to stop those things is to decide to repent. It's amazing what we will tolerate in ourselves but condemn in our wives or in our husbands. It's all right if we do it, but God help them if they step out of line. Today is the day of decision. Now is the time. You can decide inside of yourself right now and say, "I'm going to stop it right now. Father, I repent. I am sorry."

"Repent," in the Bible, means to do an about-face. You are traveling in one direction, and you say, "I'm making a mistake. I'm sinning." You stop, you do an about-face, then you go the other way. You had been going the devil's way, but you turn around and go God's way. That's what repentance is.

The power of decision-making is the most liberating thing you can know in your life. It will set you free. There is peace in making decisions. I want my will to decide for God. I want my ministry, I want my marriage, I want my thoughts, I want my relationships all ordered according to the will of God, so that I have that peace inside that lets me walk with God in faith. The Bible says, *"Beloved, if our heart condemn us not, then have we confidence toward God"* (1 John 3:21). If I'm out of God's will because of decisions I've made, I cannot know faith. And I cannot know the power of God inside because I have forcibly made decisions that move me out of God's will.

Every Decision Is Important

Even little decisions can change your life. Let me illustrate. After the death of my late wife, I felt impressed by the Spirit to wait for two years before I even considered remarriage. In September of 1984, my friend Don Moen and I were flying to Tulsa when Don leaned across the aisle of the plane. He said, "Terry, the two-year time period is up this month. Are you ready to get married?"

I had to make a decision. I had been making it, but had never admitted it to myself. I was surprised to hear my own voice say to him, "Yes, I am."

He asked, "Do you know who you want to marry?"

"No, I have no idea," I replied.

He asked, "What kind of wife are you looking for?"

I answered, "A widow. Someone who has gone through something similar to what I have experienced. I could minister to her, she could minister to me."

He said, "All right. Let's pray." He reached his hand across the aisle and began to pray out loud. For the benefit of anyone on the plane who didn't know what we were praying about, he announced, "Lord, Terry wants a wife. He's asked for a widow. With his schedule, she is going to have to live in Tulsa, and we ask that you make it soon." Then he opened his eyes and said, "Do you agree?"

With everyone looking at me, I didn't dare do anything else but agree! So I said, "Yes, I agree." (Really, though, I was in agreement with him.)

He said, "All right, it's done." Just that quick. "All right, it's done."

Decisions, decisions! This was on Monday. On Saturday that week, I took my three children to McDonald's for breakfast. As we sat down, I saw a beautiful lady sitting at the next table. In the course of our breakfast, she got up and walked over to our table and said, "Hello, is your name Terry Law?"

I answered, "Yes, it is."

She said, "I grew up with some of the early team members of your music group, Living Sound. We went to

Sunday school together." We talked about our mutual friends, where they were and what they were doing.

I noticed she was by herself, and asked, "Where is your husband?" I wasn't subtle enough to look for a wedding ring. I had never been good at that sort of thing anyway.

She said, "Oh, he passed away some time ago."

The first feeling I felt was grief. I knew what she had gone through, and I knew the hurt and the pain. But the second feeling I had was totally different from the first. It was like my brain was being burned with a red-hot iron, and I was saying, "Lord, this is only Saturday. We just prayed on Monday. This is much too soon!"

Shirley's Decision: *Obey God!*

I want to tell you Shirley's part of the story. She was home that morning, standing at the kitchen stove preparing breakfast for her two children. She had scrambled the eggs and was waiting for the porridge to thicken.

Suddenly, the Spirit of God came on her, and God said, *"Go to McDonald's."* Can you believe that God would ever say that to anybody?

She shook it off and said, "No, this can't be. Why would I want to go to McDonald's? This is just me thinking something." She had never been to McDonald's for breakfast, so it wasn't as if she were craving something from the menu! As she stood there, she heard the words again, *"Go to McDonald's."* The urge became overwhelming: she knew she had to do it. She had to make a decision.

She told her children to get dressed. In the car on the way over, her oldest daughter, Marie, broke down and started to cry. She said, "Mommy, when we go to McDonald's, it reminds me of daddy."

Shirley stopped the car. She wanted to turn around and go home, but she couldn't do it. She had made a decision. So she said, "Let's pray."

When they finished praying, Marie looked up, and with tears in her eyes, she said, *"Mommy, God is going to give us a new daddy, isn't He?"*

In the Spirit, Shirley knew it was true. She told me that when I walked into McDonald's with three children, all she could say was "Oh, *no.*"

Terry's Story: *The Smallest Decision*

There is a principle in this story that is very important. I want to tell you what happened to me that morning. I had a habit of asking our children where they wanted to go for breakfast. Sometimes we'd take a vote, sometimes I'd just say, "Scotty, you do it," or "Misty, you do it," or "Rebecca, you do it."

When we got in the car that morning, I said, "Where do you want to go for breakfast?" Misty said, "Denny's." Rebecca said, "No, daddy, it's my turn. I think we ought to go to McDonald's."

I said, "Okay, Becca, it's your turn. We'll go to McDonald's this morning."

You see, it was the smallest decision. Shirley's decision was a big one: God was thumping her on the head. Mine was a little one: the kids were talking to me from the back seat.

One little decision changed my life. She had two children, I had three. God blessed us with another little girl,

Laurie Ann, and we now have a beautiful family of six children. The Bible says blessed is the man whose quiver is full of many arrows. So I am blessed!

The Decision to Be Well

I am showing you the power of decisions. You make decisions about so many things in your life. Forgiveness is a decision, and repentance is a decision. Did you know that health and healing are also decisions that you make?

You may be waiting for an evangelist to come and pray for you so you can be healed, someone who is operating in the gift of faith or the gift of healing. Primarily that is the way Pentecostals and Charismatics look to God for healing. They wait for someone with a healing gift to come to town. And there is no question: God does heal that way.

God heals that way in my meetings. I operate in the gift of healing. It is not something I boast about; it is something I have faith for, and when I speak healing to the sick, they get healed.

I was talking with a well-known talk-show host in the United States who has a daily Christian program. He told me very honestly, "Terry, when you come on my program, we have more responses over the telephone from people who are healed when you speak healing into the television set. People get healed all over the country."

I said, "Praise the Lord for that." I know why it happens. It happens because I operate and flow in the gift of the evangelist, and the gift of healing is a part of the equipment of the New Testament evangelist.

Healing: Three Delivery Systems

God has three delivery systems for healing. You can get it from doctors, or you can get it through the gift of the healing evangelist. But if it doesn't come in either one of those ways, you can still be healed, because the healing power of God is in His Word. God's Word has the healing properties necessary to heal your body. But you have to make up your mind whether you want to get healed badly enough.

Earlier, when I wrote about the power of the Word of God, I explained that the angel Gabriel said to Mary, "Every word that God speaks contains the power for its own fulfillment." The Bible, the Word of God, has power in it to heal you and keep you healthy. You have to make the decision whether to believe the Bible or not.

Many people have never decided that. They think healing is something God stores up in heaven somewhere. But you were healed 2,000 years ago at the cross when Jesus Christ paid the price for your healing! It was done then! And the only thing separating you from your healing is a decision. You must make up your mind you were healed through Jesus at the cross. You can make that decision by determining to go to the Word and staying with the Word until the Word heals you.

Escape From Death

In 1988, I learned first-hand about the healing power of the gospel. I had not been feeling well and had gone to see the doctor. I knew something was wrong the minute they drew blood out of my arm. The blood was dark and thick. You could almost see the high sugar content in it. The lab processed the blood and sent the report back. The doctor was amazed at the results.

"That's one of the highest blood sugar readings I've seen," he said. "Your sugar level is 1,089 milligrams per deciliter. Usually people with levels over 700 go into a coma."

Fear hit me in the pit of my stomach. I could hear the enemy's taunt in my mind: "This disease will kill you."

I remembered there was a history of diabetes on my father's side of the family. His mother had died of a heart attack brought on by sugar diabetes. My aunt, an uncle, and several cousins also have the disease.

The enemy kept mocking me. "You have picked up a genetic weakness in your blood. You will have to inject yourself with needles for the rest of your life. Your body has lost its health."

At that point, I had to make one of the most crucial decisions of my life.

I looked at the doctor and asked a question: "Have you ever seen anyone healed of sugar diabetes?"

"I can't say that I have," he replied.

"Doctor," I said, "I'm your first case then." I had decided to believe God for my healing!

They put me in a hospital room, where insulin was fed intravenously into my body. I was monitored carefully by nurses who checked my blood-sugar level regularly.

When he received the news, Oral Roberts called and prayed for my healing. Richard Roberts and Billy Joe Daugherty also prayed with me. I received numerous calls from other pastors and friends who had heard of my plight. I knew I was undergirded by prayer.

I asked Shirley to get me cassette tapes on healing. The Hagins sent over a boxful. I listened to those tapes by the hour, especially one containing nothing but Bible verses about healing. Even when I awoke in the middle of the night, I would play it over and over.

"Faith cometh by hearing," said the Apostle Paul, *"and hearing by the word of God"* (Rom. 10:17). That's just what happened to me. As I listened to those tapes, meditating on the Word of God, I'm convinced that faith in His Word rose up inside of me to heal me.

I will never forget the morning. It was 7:30 A.M., Sunday, October 2, 1988.

As I listened to the healing Scriptures, one in particular seemed to speak to me. I turned off the cassette player and opened my Bible to Mark 11:24: *"Therefore I say unto you, What things soever ye desire, when ye pray, believe that ye receive them, and ye shall have them."*

Over the years, I had read that verse scores of times and had heard many sermons preached on it. But on this particular occasion, I sensed the Holy Sprit saying, *"Your healing is in that verse."* I read the verse aloud. I meditated on it. I examined each phrase.

Then I saw something I'd never noticed before: *"When ye pray, believe that ye receive."* I sensed the Spirit was saying to me, *"You must believe that you receive when you pray."*

I realized that I shouldn't believe the answer would come sometime in the future; I had to believe that I would receive it the moment I asked for it. If I believed I would receive when I prayed, it would be mine.

Then another verse came to mind: *"Who his own self bare our sins in his own body on the tree, that we, being dead to sins, should live unto righteousness, By whose stripes ye were healed"* (1 Pet. 2:24). I've always believed that our healing was provided for in the Atonement, but I was struck by the use of the past tense in that phrase: *"Ye were healed."* My healing was accomplished in the past.

At this point, I asked God a question: "Lord, if I was healed at the cross by the stripes inflicted on Jesus, what is this sugar diabetes doing in my body now?"

I sensed a quiet reply: *"You were healed at the cross — so do something about the sugar diabetes now."*

Then I saw it. The healing was mine; it had already been provided for, but I had to receive it actively now by faith.

I sat up in bed and said aloud: "Sugar diabetes, hear the Word of the Lord. This verse says *'what things soever ye desire'* — I desire healing now. It also says, *'when ye pray, believe that ye receive'* — I believe I receive the healing now when I pray. Healing is mine by faith. So, sugar diabetes, get out of my body and stay out of my body. I am healed in Jesus' name!"

The joy of the Lord welled up inside of me. I got out of bed with the intravenous tubes still inserted in my arm and carefully walked around the bedside cart with one hand in the air, praising the Lord that it was done. At that point, I didn't care what the symptoms showed; I knew I received healing when I prayed.

When the doctor came, he tested my sugar level again and noticed a significant downturn. The doctor insisted that they continue to administer the insulin, which I thought was a good idea. But he did diminish the doses gradually.

After three weeks, I was off of insulin and pills. After about six weeks, the doctor phoned me and announced, *"Terry, healing is breaking out all over in your body."*

"Thank you, doctor, for those words," I said. *"I knew it, but I wanted to hear you say it."*

If Satan ever puts a dreaded disease on your body, go to the Word of God. As you meditate on healing Scriptures over and over, faith will rise in your spirit until you are convinced that you were healed through Jesus' sacrifice at Calvary. Command that disease to go. Stay with the Word until the disease leaves. That disease cannot hold on to you because you have made a decision to be healed. *See, faith begins with a decision.*

Romans 10:17 says, *"So then faith cometh by hearing, and hearing by the word of God."* Notice the first four words, *"So then faith cometh...."* Faith is coming to you. Faith is proceeding to you. You can have faith, but it never happens until you make the decision to pursue it. To do that, you've got to go to the Word, and you've got to stay with the Word until the Word heals you.

I realize these are strong words, but I can back them up with the Word of God. Proverbs 4:20-22 says:

My son, attend to my words; incline thine ear unto my sayings. Let them not depart from thine eyes; keep them in the midst of thine heart. For they are life unto those that find them, and health to all their flesh. [One translation says, *"My words are medicine to all their flesh."*]

The Word of God is health for you. It is health to your flesh. But you must make a decision whether you want to get healed. As soon as you make the decision, you are on the pathway, and the Word of God will heal you.

You say, "That's pretty radical." Well, I can back that up with a text, too: *"This day I call heaven and earth as witnesses against you that I have set before you life and death, blessing and curses. Now choose life, so that you and your children may live"* (Deut. 30:19, NIV).

And I say to you now: therefore choose life, choose health, choose forgiveness, choose repentance—that both you and your children may live.

In the outer court, you deal with the objective facts of what God did for you through the blood of Jesus and through the Word. In the Holy Place, you come to God with your will and your decisions, and you submit them to Him. As you bring your will into line with God's plan for you, you will be able to say, as Jesus said, "Not my will, but thine be done."

Now, as a person submitted to the presence of God, you are in a position to see the manifestation of the power of God in your life!

6

The Battle of the Mind
The Golden Candlestick

FOR MANY BELIEVERS, THE MIND is the biggest roadblock to enjoying the presence of the Lord. The mind will do everything it can to stay in control and to resist the power of the Holy Spirit. Yet, to get into the presence of God, you need a mind that can flow with the Holy Spirit, that can receive the revelation that God will give you when you come into His divine presence in the Holy of Holies.

When the priest walked through the first veil into the Holy Place, he stepped into a dim, enclosed space. Heavy curtains kept natural, outdoor light from penetrating. The only light shone out from the golden candlestick. It stood on the floor, on the left side of the Holy Place, opposite the table of showbread. It was made with a central shaft and six additional branches, three branches on each side of the central shaft. The branches and the central shaft were beautifully decorated with golden cups shaped like almond blossoms. The entire candlestick was "beaten" or hammered out of a single piece of gold, weighing over 100 pounds.

Seven lamps were mounted on the candlestick, one on each of the six branches, and one on the central shaft. When these lamps were lit, the glow from the flames lit up the Holy Place (Exod. 25:31-37).

Illuminated by the Holy Spirit

On our way into the presence of God, we have dealt with sin, we have been renewed by the Word, and we have learned to give the sacrifice of thanksgiving and praise. At the table of showbread, we have learned to submit our wills to God's plan. I believe that the golden candlestick is the place where God intends for us to deal with our minds. As we approach God's presence, we realize that just as natural light isn't enough to light up the Holy Place, natural thinking is inadequate to understand God's ways. We need to be illuminated by the Holy Spirit.

As the candlestick was hammered out of a single piece of gold, our minds also need to be shaped by the Holy Spirit in order to be able to receive the Word of God. Once shaped, our minds can be of service to us and others. A renewed mind is on fire and it gives forth light.

The Carnal Mind

Unfortunately, many believers never renew their minds; rather, they allow their minds to remain carnal. Paul says, in Romans 8:7, *"The carnal mind is enmity against God; for it is not subject to the law of God, neither indeed can be."* Paul says, the carnal mind fights against God. A carnal mind hinders us from coming into the presence of the Lord. Most of the time your unrenewed mind does not want your spirit to be supreme inside of you. Your natural mind will struggle to control you, and will resist the power of the Holy Spirit. It will fight with your spirit whenever it is time to take a step of faith. It is an enemy of the things of God.

Casting Down Imaginations

The Bible says, in 2 Corinthians 10:3-5, *"For though we walk in the flesh, we do not war after the flesh: (For the weapons of our warfare are not carnal, but mighty through God to the pulling down of strong holds;) Casting down imaginations, and every high thing* [some translations say, "every proud thing"] *that exalteth itself against the knowledge of God, and bringing into captivity every thought to the obedience of Christ."*

In the previous chapter, we discussed how your imagination and your thoughts are a primary target of attacks from the devil. We saw how the devil uses thoughts to make us feel guilty, to make our bodies sick, and to distract us from seeking God. We discussed how your will was the boss, and how you could tell your mind to be quiet.

These verses tell us that we've got to cast down imaginations, we've got to bring every thought into captivity. That's the first step in getting our minds ready to receive what God has to say.

The Renewing of Your Mind

However, shutting your mind off is not God's ultimate plan for you. He wants you to take the next step: renewing your mind. In Romans 12, Paul says, *"Be not conformed to this world; but be ye transformed by the renewing of your mind."* You've got to do something about the carnal mind. You've got to renew it, transform it.

The word "transform" there is *"metamorphose"* in the original Greek, a very interesting word. A metamorphosis is what happens when a caterpillar turns into a butterfly. Do you like caterpillars? Do you like butterflies? Caterpillars are ugly creatures; butterflies are beautiful. Essentially Paul was saying your carnal mind is ugly; it's a caterpillar, but God wants to renew your carnal mind and get it prepared to hear the voice of God in the presence of the Lord.

Some Christians get confused and think that any intellectual activity is against faith. This is not the case. God made your mind. He wants you to use it. But first, it must be renewed so it can receive the things freely given by Him.

Search the Scriptures. Meditate on them. You will never dig so deep that you will make God nervous. He is not afraid of your intelligence! His Word is consistent through and through.

The Human Mind and the Human Spirit

In 1 Corinthians 2:9-16, Paul gives us step-by-step instructions on how to prepare our minds to follow after God. Let's go through this passage, verse by verse :

"But as it is written, Eye hath not seen, nor ear heard, neither have entered into the heart of man...." The word *heart* is interesting: it is the word *"cardia"* in the Greek. It doesn't refer to the organ we call the heart. Rather, it refers to either the human spirit or to the human mind. Sometimes it's one; sometimes it's the other. You must examine the context to be sure which it is in each particular case.

Let me give you an example. Do you remember when the man with the palsy was let down through a hole in the roof? Jesus saw the faith of his friends and healed him. The Bible says the scribes and Pharisees began to reason about what had happened. *"But when Jesus perceived their thoughts,* he answering said unto them, *What reason ye in your hearts?*" (Luke 5:22). The word for *heart* in this verse is also *"cardia,"* yet it is clear from the context that the men were thinking and reasoning. Their intellects were involved. In this Scripture, *"cardia"* refers to the mind of man rather than the spirit of man.

I believe *"cardia"* in 1 Corinthians 2:9 is also referring to the mind of man. In essence, Paul is saying, "Your eyes have not seen, nor have your ears heard, neither have entered into your mind the things which God has prepared for them that love Him." The last phrase, "the things which God has prepared for them that love Him," is vital to your understanding of the next few verses.

Heavenly Minded

When I was growing up, I memorized these verses in Sunday school. I always believed that Paul was talking about the things in heaven. I thought he was saying my eyes could not see the things in heaven, my ears couldn't hear them, and my mind couldn't even conceive of the beautiful things God had prepared for me up there.

But more recently, I began to study the rest of the verses in this passage, and I began to realize that this verse was not talking about heaven at all. This verse was talking about things God has prepared for us right here on the earth, and they are available to everyone in the Kingdom of God right now. I started getting excited as I began to realize that God has prepared some wonderful things for the Body of Christ.

What God Has Prepared for You

Do you love God? Then there's a whole wonderful assortment of delights out there that God has prepared for you: delicious good things on the table of the Lord, delectable provisions that will satisfy the most discriminating palate. But you've got a problem: your eyes can't see them, your ears can't hear them, and your mind can't understand them. How do you find out about what God has prepared for you? How do you pull up to the table and partake of all God has put there?

Our answer is found in verse 10: *"But God hath revealed them unto us by his Spirit."* Notice the word "hath" is in the past tense. These good things were first revealed to mankind by the Word of God. And now the Holy Spirit is in the process of revealing to each of us those same powerful and mighty things that God has prepared for those who love Him.

The Holy Spirit wants to show us. It's His job to do so. In John 16:14, Jesus said the Holy Spirit *"will receive of mine, and shall show it unto you."* The Holy Spirit sheds light on the truth and illuminates our minds.

Some scholars have suggested that the seven lamps of the golden candlestick correspond to the seven spirits of God mentioned in Revelation 3:1 and listed in Isaiah 11:2: the Spirit of the Lord, the spirit of wisdom and understanding, the spirit of counsel and might, the spirit of knowledge and of the fear of the Lord. It's interesting to note how many of these deal with mental activity, with functions of the mind. Only with the help of the Holy Spirit can we start to understand the things God has prepared for us.

Redemption's Gifts

I believe the "things which God has prepared for them that love Him" were prepared by God when Jesus Christ died for us on the cross. You will never truly enter into the mighty and powerful things of your redemption until you go back to the cross and find out the price that was paid for you and what God bought for you with the price of Jesus' death.

There are eight primary things I am going to name that were purchased for you at the cross. They are gifts from God to you, the things God has prepared for you. You should meditate on these things day by day, because these wonderful things are already set out for you on the table of the Lord. They are there for you, even though your eyes can't see them, your ears can't hear them, and your mind doesn't totally understand them.

The first thing God did in Christ was to give us remission of sins (Eph. 1:7). Jesus took our punishment and gave us the remission of our sins. "Remission" means that our sins were blotted out completely. God has no memory of your sin because the blood of Jesus has cleansed you completely. There is no record of your past. It has been remitted. Praise the Lord!

The second thing God has prepared concerns our health. Jesus took sickness and pain that we might receive health and healing (1 Pet. 2:24, Matt. 8:17, Isa. 53:4). There is a difference between the two: healing is the halfway point, while health, divine health, is God's best for us. Both are on the table of the Lord, prepared by God for His children. Although we can't see it or hear it, the Spirit of God knows it's there, and He is going to show it to us.

The next good thing on the table of the Lord is called righteousness. Jesus, who knew no sin, became sin for us *"that we might be made the righteousness of God in him"* (2 Cor. 5:21). When you receive the imputed righteousness of God, you are recreated in your inner man. You receive the actual nature of God himself. When God sees you, He sees Jesus' righteousness. You have been made righteous. Declare it. Say, "I am righteous!"

The fourth thing God has prepared for them that love Him is life. Jesus tasted death and He gave us life — three kinds of life: physical life, spiritual life, and eternal life. All three forms of life have been given to us.

The fifth thing God has prepared for them that love Him is abundance. *"Though he* [Jesus] *was rich, yet for your sakes he became poor, so that you through his poverty might become rich"* (2 Cor. 8:9b, NIV). Please study this verse carefully. Abundance in the Bible is the opposite of hunger, thirst, nakedness, and want, the curses listed in Deuteronomy 28:48. Abundance is waiting for you at the table of the Lord.

If you say, "I don't believe God wants to prosper the Church," then you have never read your Bible! Jesus Christ died on the cross. He was made poor. You cannot read through the account of the Crucifixion and then read the curses in Deuteronomy 28, without realizing that when Jesus Christ was on the cross, He was absolutely poor. He was hungry, He was naked, He was thirsty, He had want of all things.

Jesus was made poor that we, through His poverty, might be made rich. He paid the price for it, and it's on the table of the Lord. If you don't want to come to the table, that's your problem. I'm going to go there and receive in Jesus' name. Hallelujah!

The sixth thing God has prepared for them that love Him is to share in His glory. Jesus took our shame so we could share His glory. He endured the cross, despising the shame (Heb. 12:2). Shame is what we experience as an absolute sense of unworthiness, and a complete lack of self-esteem.

Shame is a common result of sexual abuse in children. A counselor in Tulsa told me recently that twenty-five percent of women and over ten percent of men were sexually abused when they were younger. That abuse has created a tremendous reservoir of shame in our country.

Jesus experienced absolute shame when they hung Him naked on that cross. He was exposed to the gaze of the soldiers who jeered and mocked. He took all of this in our behalf.

In exchange, He offers us a share in His glory. He shares with us the glory that belongs to Him by eternal right (Heb. 2:10).

The seventh thing God has prepared for them that love Him is acceptance into the family of God. Jesus took our rejection so that we could be accepted.

Rejection is everywhere in our society. Rejection happens in divorce — when a person rejects a spouse. It happens when a parent rejects a child. It may occur because of a failure to simply show love and acceptance. The pastor of a very large church in Atlanta, who has a Ph.D. in counseling, told me recently, "Eighty percent of my counseling could be summed up as originating in shame and rejection."

Jesus was rejected on the cross. The Father made Him to be sin with our sin (2 Cor. 5:21). Because the Father is holy, He had to turn His back on the Son because our sin was on Him. When this happened, Jesus felt rejection in an extreme form. He cried, "My God, my God, why hast thou forsaken me?" Jesus understands our feeling of rejection. He has made a way for us to be accepted into God's family. According to Romans 8:15, we have received the Spirit of sonship and can now address God as *Abba,* which means Papa or Daddy.

The eighth thing God has prepared for them that love Him is the blessing of God. Jesus was made a curse so that we might receive the blessing (Gal. 3:13-14). Deuteronomy 28:1-14 lists the incredible blessings of God. These are what God has prepared for you: fruitfulness in your family; protection, with angels watching over you; direction — the Word of God to guide you day by day; victory over your enemies and over the devil; success in your business and in your family; honor among men, favor, riches, and dominion. These are just some of the blessings that are on the table of the Lord. They are the things God has prepared for them that love Him.

Do you like to have favor? I do! Recently I was scheduled to speak in Lakeland, Florida. I had to fly from Tulsa to Tampa late Saturday evening. My Tulsa plane taxied onto the runway and began to accelerate. Then, suddenly, the pilot hit the brakes. A light was malfunctioning in the cockpit and had to be fixed. We taxied onto the runway the second time, and again, the brakes were applied. We had a flat tire. The third time onto the runway, the plane became airborne and headed for Dallas.

I checked my watch and realized I would miss my connecting flight. Everyone around me was upset. Businessmen were cursing. I chose to ask God and believe for favor. I remained calm and firm in my faith.

When I disembarked at Dallas, I met the lady who had connecting gate information. I told her I was going to Tampa. "Oh," she said, "Sir, today is your lucky day! That flight is slightly delayed. It is just two gates down on your left." I ran to the gate and down the tunnel to the plane.

A stewardess saw me and asked, "Are you Terry Law?"

"Yes, " I replied.

She said, "We've been waiting for you," and ushered me to my seat. Now that is favor! It is part of our inheritance. The Father loves it when you believe Him for the little things!

"But as it is written, Eye hath not seen, nor ear heard, neither have entered into the heart of man, the things which God hath prepared for them that love him. But God hath revealed them unto us by his Spirit" (1 Cor. 2:9). You cannot really understand this portion of the Scriptures until you understand the eight gifts I've outlined. Say this out loud: "These are the things God has prepared for me because I love Him. He has prepared remission of sins, He has prepared healing and health, He has prepared righteousness, He has prepared life, He has prepared abundance, He has prepared glory, He has prepared a family, He has prepared blessing, and they are all mine in Jesus' name."

What If It's Not Working?

Sometimes people come up to me and say, "Preacher, I've heard others teach this for years. But somehow I'm not experiencing these blessings in my life. What is wrong?

How can I sit up to the table and start enjoying what God has given me?"

Let's go right back to verse 9. Your eyes can't see it; your ears can't hear it. Your natural mind cannot understand it. So how do we partake of these things first-hand? Our answer is found in verse 10: *"But God hath revealed them unto us by his Spirit...."* These things are revealed only through the Holy Spirit. If you are going to understand these things, the only way to pick them up is to pick them up in the spirit.

You are a triune being. You live in a body and you have a soul, composed of three parts: will, intelligence, and emotion. But you are essentially a spirit. Before you were born again, your spirit was dead, darkened, outside of God. You were called in the Bible, "the children of wrath."

But when you were born again, God, the Holy Spirit, breathed on your human spirit, and your human spirit came alive with the life of God. That is why Paul could say, *"If any man be in Christ, he is a new creature, old things are passed away; behold, all things are become new"* (2 Cor. 5:17). You are made a new creation, a new creature in Christ. That means your human spirit has come alive by the Holy Spirit. Say this out loud: "My human spirit is alive by the Holy Spirit. And it is my human spirit that shows me the things God has prepared for me." Hallelujah!

We must get to a place where we start to hear what our spirit is saying. Look at 1 Corinthians 2:11 carefully: *"For what man knoweth the things of a man, save the spirit of man which is in him?"* I know a whole lot of people who spend a great deal of time and money on psychiatrists and on other professionals, trying to find out what is wrong with them. I am not saying that counseling is not good; it can be a very valuable tool of the Holy Spirit.

But according to this verse, your spirit, your inner man, knows what is wrong with you. If you've got a problem, your regenerated human spirit is aware of it. *"For what man knoweth the things of a man, save the spirit of man which is in him?"* Your human spirit knows what you need. It knows what you're longing for. If you're lonely, your spirit knows. If you're weary, it knows that, too. Your spirit knows you intimately, it knows all about you.

Now look at the next part of the verse: *"...even so the things of God knoweth no man, but the Spirit of God."* The Holy Spirit knows the things of God. He knows all the wonderful things God has prepared for them that love Him. The Holy Spirit knows the divine supply.

We need a link between the Holy Spirit and your human spirit, between the One who knows the divine supply and the one who understands your deepest needs and longings. So our challenge is to get the Holy Spirit and our spirit in communion so that the Holy Spirit can start ministering the things God has prepared for them that love Him to our human spirit, and our spirit can start understanding and partaking of what the Holy Spirit has for us.

Let's go on to verse twelve: *"Now we have received, not the spirit of the world, but the spirit which is of God; that we might know the things that are freely given to us of God."* Say this out loud: "I don't have the spirit of the world. Here's what I've got, I've got the Spirit which is of God. And here is why I've got the Spirit which is of God: that I might know the things that are freely given to me by God."

Why do you have the Holy Spirit? So that you might know. Know what? *"...the things that are freely given to us of God."* That is why you have the Holy Spirit! He is trying to show you healing. He is trying to show you blessing. He is trying to show you prosperity. He is trying to show you the good things of God. He is trying to get it through to you.

Verse thirteen says, *"Which things also we speak, not in the words which man's wisdom teacheth, but which the Holy Ghost teacheth...."* Apparently the things freely given by God were the subject of Paul's preaching all the time. Paul must have been a prosperity preacher and a healing preacher. He must have preached about blessing, life, and righteousness. *"Which things also we speak...."* He says, "I preach this all the time."

He goes on to say, "But I don't do it with the words of man's wisdom. I talk to you all the time about these things, but I speak to you in the words that the Holy Spirit gives me." Until you realize that the Holy Spirit, the Spirit of God, in you, is waiting there, yearning to let you know all that God has for you, you will be missing out.

The Problem of the Mind

In verse fourteen, Paul describes the problem of the mind: *"But the natural man receiveth not the things of the Spirit of God, for they are foolishness unto him, neither can he know them, because they are spiritually discerned."* What is Paul talking about? He is talking about the mind of your natural man, your carnal mind. It will never understand the things of the Spirit of God because it does not want to know them. It is carnally oriented: it believes what your eyes see and what your ears hear. Your natural mind can't understand the blessings of God, but the Holy Spirit is trying to show them to you.

He's in the business of showing you remission of sins, healing, righteousness, life, fruitfulness, success, honor, riches, financial abundance, physical life, spiritual life, and eternal life. These things are all yours. The only reason you are not walking in healing or prosperity is because your mind won't receive them.

Your mind oftentimes will reject what the Holy Spirit brings up in your human spirit. The Holy Spirit is trying to open your eyes. But your natural mind says, "No, prosperity is not for today. Healing is not for today. No, that's not for me."

This is the reason why when you talk about healing to a lot of people, they will say, "That's not for me. Don't you know healing was done away with when the last apostle died? God doesn't heal people today. If He heals, He should have healed Sister Jones, who died of cancer, because she was the most spiritual person in our church." The natural mind rejects what God's Word says. It cannot understand without the illumination of the Holy Spirit.

But we have tapped into a new source of understanding. We have a new source of revelation, called the Holy Spirit. There are times when you've got to tell your natural man to be quiet. At such times, you must read the Word of God to your natural man and tell him he doesn't understand, but your spirit understands. Tell your mind to quit listening to what the world says and what your senses say, and start picking up what your spirit is saying. Once your mind picks up what the Holy Spirit is saying to your spirit, you're going to start walking in the blessings of God.

Moving the Mind From Carnal to Spiritual

You have the Holy Spirit inside you, and the Holy Spirit inside you knows the things God has prepared for them that love Him. He is continually trying to show these truths to you; in fact, He has already revealed them to you in your spirit.

So here is the question: How can you get your carnal mind to shut up so you can start hearing what the Holy Spirit is saying to you by way of your human spirit?

In 1 Corinthians 14, we discover a great insight. Verse 2 says: *"For he that speaketh in an unknown tongue speaketh not unto men, but unto God, for no man understandeth him; howbeit in the spirit he speaketh mysteries."*

Now move down to verse 13: *"Wherefore let him that speaketh in an unknown tongue pray that he may interpret."* The person who speaks is to pray that he will interpret what he has spoken. We have heard this principle applied in a church setting, but for now, I'd like you to see how it can be used on a personal level as well. Notice verse 14: *"For if I pray in an unknown tongue, my spirit prayeth, but my understanding is unfruitful."* My spirit is praying mysteries, but my mind does not understand it. I don't want my mind to be unfruitful. I want to understand.

Now verse 15: *"What is it then? I will pray with the spirit, and I will pray with the understanding also, I will sing with the spirit, and I will sing with the understanding also."* Notice how Paul puts this. He says, "I'm going to do it this way. I'm not just going to talk in tongues, I'm going to interpret the tongues."

A couple of verses later, Paul says, *"I thank my God, I speak with tongues more than ye all."* Why did he say that? Because he had discovered the tremendous blessing that speaking in tongues had brought to him.

When you speak in tongues, your spirit is praying and speaking mysteries. If you want to understand the mysteries that your spirit is praying, don't just speak in tongues, but pray that you may interpret also. Why? So that your understanding will begin to get hold of what your spirit has been crying out to say to you, but your mind has been too numb to understand!

The Missing Link

We have to see this! It's something that has been missed by many in the Charismatic and Pentecostal movements. Not many of us have understood the reason why God gave a prayer language to the Body of Christ. This next truth I'm going to share with you is a real blockbuster. If you will receive it, I guarantee that your mind will be ready to come into the presence of God.

As I mentioned in a previous chapter, after my late wife's death, I spent some time with Oral Roberts in Tulsa. He called me to his office and we spent much time in the Word together. I'll never forget one part of our conversation. We were on the seventh floor of the Learning Resources Center, which is above the rest of the campus. When you walk to the window, you can see all of the buildings of Oral Roberts University.

Brother Roberts took me to the window and said, "See that building over there?"

"Yes," I replied.

"I was praying in the Holy Spirit, and I began to interpret back what the Holy Spirit was saying through me in tongues," he explained. "When I began to interpret it back, the Holy Spirit said, *'You build that building,'* so I built it."

I said, "You're kidding me."

He said, "Oh, no. Every building on this campus came from the Holy Spirit in the same way."

"But, brother," I said, "I have been taught as a classical Pentecostal that you open yourself to error if you start praying in tongues and interpreting back your own tongues and act like you've got a hotline to glory. I have seen a lot of people get into error and get messed up doing that. Are you sure about this?"

He said, "Terry, before God, it's true. The Holy Spirit revealed to me what Paul is saying in 1 Corinthians 14. When I began to trust the interpretation of my prayer language, all of a sudden, my mind started to get flooded with the good things of God. I couldn't believe what was coming up out of my spirit. It totally blew my mind."

I believe that's what we need. We need to have our minds blown, completely blown, by the Holy Spirit.

But I am one who says, "In the mouth of two or three witnesses shall every word be established." The next week, I spent some time with Kenneth Hagin, and I brought up the subject to him.

I said, "Brother Hagin, I know that you pray in the spirit a lot, and that you interpret back on occasion, but Oral Roberts told me that every building on that campus was given to him by the Holy Spirit after praying in the spirit and then interpreting back. He told me he's been doing this for thirty years."

Brother Hagin smiled at me and said, "I've been doing it for forty."

I said, "You've *got* to be kidding!"

He said, "Oh, no. From the earliest times of my ministry, I would be praying in the Holy Spirit, and according to what Paul said in 1 Corinthians 14, my understanding was unfruitful, I was speaking mysteries. I began to hunger to understand what the Holy Spirit was trying to say to me, so I began to pray to interpret. When I began to pray to interpret, the Holy Spirit began to bring up in me the good things of God. My whole ministry is based on that. Every major revelation of my ministry has come out of that."

I said, "Oh, what has the Body of Christ been missing?"

I do believe I need to add a word of caution here. I think it is very possible for someone to pray in the Spirit and then interpret out of their mind. It is very possible to get into error here. I believe it is important to test what you receive with other members of the Body of Christ. There are many times when your prayer language is simply praise to God, but there are other times when we are to pray to interpret. The more you walk in this, the more sensitive you become as to what the Spirit is saying to do.

Speaking It Out

A month and a half later, I was in my bedroom praying in the Holy Spirit, when the anointing came on me, and I launched out. I said, "I'm going to do it!" I began to interpret what I'd been praying in the Holy Spirit.

Here's what came out of me as the Holy Spirit said; *"I have taught you a sacrifice of praise through the horrible experience* [of your wife's death], *and now I am going to send you to my people. I am going to send you to the Body of Christ. If you will lead them into my presence with a sacrifice of praise, I'm going to heal the sick, I'm going to deliver the oppressed, and I'm going to save the lost."*

I spoke that back to myself in my own bedroom. When I got up off my knees that day, something had lit a fire way down deep inside of me. I called my office and said to my music director, Don Moen, "I want every song that Living Sound has ever sung that is not expressly praise and worship put on the shelf. The Holy Spirit has given us a mandate. We are going into the ministry of praise and worship. Every song we sing will be praise and worship. When we lead congregations into praise, and into the presence of God, we will see a manifestation of healing, and bodies are going to be set free."

I said, "Get ready for the first crusade. I don't care where it is."

"It's going to take two or three months," he said.

"Okay, whatever it takes, get ready," I said, "because we're going to see healing happen in our first praise and worship meeting."

Following the Holy Spirit's Instructions

We made the plans. We decided to have our first crusade in Woodward, Oklahoma. It is very close to the end of the world, way out in the Panhandle. It is very flat, dry country, except that it was the month of February. When we drove into town, they were having the worst blizzard they had had in twelve years. The announcer on the radio was telling everybody, "Please stay home. Don't come out tonight. It's very dangerous on the streets, and nobody should be out driving." This was the night for our first healing crusade with praise and worship. It was certainly a strong stimulus for my faith!

I also had an entire group of young people with me who had never seen healing happen in the midst of praise and worship. Nobody had ever demonstrated it to them. I had put my faith on the line. I had told them, "When we get in there and we start to praise the Lord, you're going to watch people get healed all over the room! God said it to me in my bedroom!"

If you decide to put into practice what I'm telling you, don't do it half-heartedly. If you're going to get into it, go into it all the way. You must be willing to follow what the Holy Spirit says to you, or after a while He's not going to speak to you anymore!

When we arrived, about seventy people had shown up in a large auditorium that seated 600 people. The loneliest place in the world is in a large auditorium with seventy people. The praise and worship echoed off the walls. Nobody was that excited about raising their hands because there were very few people and they were all scattered around the massive room. Nobody sat together. It was the worst situation you ever saw in your life for praise and worship.

I watched them. They got their hands in the air, and they started to praise the Lord. There didn't seem to be that great of an anointing on the praise, but the Holy Spirit had said something to me. I came to the end of the service and I told the people, "This is what the Holy Spirit said to me three months ago in my bedroom in Tulsa. The Holy Spirit said if I would lead you into the presence of God in praise and worship, He would heal the sick."

I took a deep breath and continued: "So we're going to watch God heal the sick right now." As I spoke, my mind was doing flip-flops!

Then I told God, "If this doesn't work tonight, I'm going out of business. These young people from our ministry will never believe me again. They've followed me for almost twenty years, and they've seen me make some mistakes, but if they see one tonight, they'll never believe me again."

After we'd praised the Lord, I said, "All right, I'm going to start to pray," and I started to pray. For the first time in my ministry, people started getting healed all over the room. The anointing came, and God started healing the sick. It came on one after another. There were incontestable healings. No one could say that it was just mind over matter. There were absolute healings done by the grace of God, and we saw them with our physical eyes.

The Holy Spirit said to me, *"See, son, I've got a whole lot of things prepared for them that love me. They're in your spirit, but you've got to get them up so your mind starts to understand what the Holy Spirit is trying to show you in your spirit. If you'll pray in the spirit and then interpret back, I will open the wealth of my kingdom to you, and I will show you what I've got planned for my Body."*

He's not just doing that for the preachers. We're not some select group that's somehow been chosen by God for special revelation. I believe what I am saying is a general principle for the entire Body of Christ.

The only way to get into the presence of God is to get your carnal mind shoved out of the way. Pray in the spirit, interpret back, and get your mind hearing what the Holy Spirit is saying. By doing this, you've made your mind submit itself. You've cast down imaginations. You've brought every thought into captivity. Captivity to what? Captivity to the Holy Spirit!

Now you're ready to move through the veil. You're ready for the glory. You're ready for the power. *Hallelujah! Glory to God!*

7

Worshiping In God's Presence
In the Holy of Holies

AT LAST YOU HAVE REACHED the golden altar of incense, and the only thing separating you from the presence of God in the Holy of Holies is the final veil. Now you release the love that's in your heart for the One who made you, redeemed you, and blesses you. Your heart-felt adoration rises up from the altar of incense. Suddenly, a divine connection is made and your praise is changed to worship, which carries you into the Holy of Holies, into the awesome presence of God.

THE GOLDEN ALTAR OF INCENSE stood in the Holy Place immediately in front of the veil. This golden altar was eighteen inches square and stood three feet high. It had a golden horn on each corner, and a crown — a rim or molding — around the top. Every morning and every evening, the priests would burn a special incense there. When the priests placed that incense on the live coals, a beautiful, fragrant, white smoke would rise up from the altar before the curtain into the Holy of Holies.

143

More Than a Feeling

The golden altar of incense represents our human emotions. The pattern given for the high priest to approach the presence of God is still significant to us: we approach the table of showbread (which represents the will) and the golden candlestick (which represents the mind) before we come to the golden altar of incense. As we come into the presence of God, it is important that we commit our wills first, and renew our minds second, before we expect our emotions to respond.

The filigreed crown around the top of the altar of incense symbolizes the crown of self-control. We are in charge of our emotions; our emotions are not in charge of us. First, make sure your will is submitted to God and your mind is renewed by praying in the spirit. Then your emotions can be trusted. We don't come with our emotions first; we cannot trust emotions that rule us. Until our wills and our intellects have been dealt with, we are not in a position to turn our emotions loose in praise and then ultimately in worship.

To Enter the Holy of Holies

The high priest could never enter the Holy of Holies and approach the presence of God without bringing two things: blood and incense. God commanded the high priest to bring blood to sprinkle upon the mercy seat and incense from the golden altar to burn before the Lord. If he tried to get into the presence of God without either one, he would be struck dead.

These are the two things that bring you to God: the awareness of the work of the blood of Jesus in your life, and your praise and worship. These are two vital components of true worship. *I cannot enter into powerful worship until I have a strong awareness of the work of the blood on behalf of Terry Law.* When I express my gratitude to God for the work of the blood of Jesus, something happens in my spirit that propels me into the area of worship.

A Sweet-Smelling Savor

God gave Moses the formula for the incense that was placed on the golden altar. It was to be compounded from four different rare spices: stacte, onycha, galbanum, and frankincense. The incense was costly; in the same way true worship is costly. Worship demands a price both of time and of discipline.

The incense also required preparation. The priest had to crush the spices into a powder and then blend them together perfectly in equal proportions. An old-fashioned word for crushing something into a powder is *contrition.* (A contriter was a machine that was used to crush rocks.) For example, talcum powder has been contrited. It has been ground so fine and so smooth that you are not even aware of what it used to be.

That is what happens in worship. For our worship to come before the Lord, it must come from a broken, contrite heart, a heart that is not full of pride. To worship we must be broken. That is the only way to get to where God is.

God Is a Jealous God

This special incense was to be used only in the Temple. The formula could not be copied for private use. If anyone did so, he was to be *"cut off from his people."* In the same way, God is jealous of your worship. That's why the first commandment is *"Thou shalt have no other gods before me"* (Exod. 20:3). Jesus said, *"Thou shalt love the Lord thy God with all thy heart"* (Matt. 22:37). God wants your worship, and He wants you to worship Him alone.

At the beginning of this book, I said to you that man is a worshiping creature. Man has to worship. He worships something: if it's not God, it's an idol. One of the greatest gods in America today is materialism: people worship their boats, their cars, their swimming pools; they worship so many of the material things of life. Spending all their time and energy to obtain and maintain all these possessions simply excludes the worship of God — they have no time or energy left!

If you've got other idols, then you're burning incense on another altar, and God won't accept that. Not at all. He demands that we offer the incense of our worship at His altar. If we do that, we will be in His presence, and He will be where we are.

The Fire of God

The fire that burned on this altar came from God. First, He kindled the fire on the altar of blood sacrifice (Lev. 9:24). When the altar of incense was first set up in the Tabernacle, God told the priest, *"Go and get the fire from the altar of blood sacrifice that I started myself. Take that divine fire and put it on the golden altar of incense. You must keep those coals alive forever."* So, live coals from the brazen altar were brought to the golden altar of incense.

There is a message here. You need a fire in your spirit, in your heart, to bring you into worship. God is not interested in dead coals. Nothing is more unsightly than coal that has been burned up and does not have any fire in it anymore. But there are a lot of believers who are just like that: they are burnt out. Worshiping God requires the fresh coals of sacrifice and meditation. It takes prayer, it takes praise, it takes time lavished on the Lord in order to come into His presence. *God wants a heart of fire.*

Yet, how many of us come to church with empty hearts, tired bodies, unopened Bibles and prayerless spirits? That is what destroys praise in most churches. It destroys worship. If you want real worship, there has to be fire on the altar. You're the only one that can bring it. Nobody can bring it for you.

Jesus became angry at the church at Laodicea, and said to them, "I wish that you were either hot or cold, but because you are only lukewarm, I am going to spit you out of my mouth" (Rev. 3:15-16, author's paraphrase). If you're going to come to Him, come to Him with a hot heart, a heart that has been in meditation and prayer and praise.

The beautiful perfumed smoke that symbolizes your praise rises up like a smoke of incense in the nostrils of God. It is that smoke that brings you through the veil and into the presence of God. When God receives the incense of your praise and introduces you to the immediacy of His presence, you have made the transition from your soul to your spirit. You've passed out of praise, and are now in worship.

What Worship Is

Exactly what is worship from a biblical perspective? How can we understand it better? The word "worship" comes from an Old English term, "worthscipe," later changed to "worschipe," and then to "worship." It speaks of the worthiness, the dignity, or the merit of a person. In fact, the English still address their judges as, "Your Worship."

When used as a verb, worship means, "paying homage, or respect, or giving great honor." The most common word for worship in the Hebrew language is *shachah*. It appears 172 times in the Old Testament, and is translated in a variety of ways: "to bow down," "to prostrate," "to stoop," "to do reverence," or "to beseech humbly." All these are outward actions associated with an attitude of humility in the heart.

The most common word for worship in the New Testament is *proskuneo* in the Greek language. It appears fifty-nine times. *Pros* means "towards," *kuneo* means "to kiss." So the meaning of the most common word for worship in the New Testament is "kissing towards."

This is quite different from the Old Testament concept of bowing and doing reverence, as kissing requires contact and intimacy. New Testament saints are beckoned to get close enough to embrace God, to love Him, to kiss Him, and to pour out adoration unto Him. It is precisely at this point that many of us draw back from the intimate nature of worship as revealed to the Church.

Beyond Definition

Beyond the simple meaning of the words, it is difficult to define what worship is, much less to prescribe how it should be done. In his *Expository Dictionary of Old and New Testament Words*, W. E. Vine says the worship of God is nowhere defined in the Scriptures. You cannot find a definition. I believe there's a reason for this: if the Bible gave us a definition, man being the way he is, would have put rules around the definition, and turned it into an empty ritual!

Defining worship is similar in difficulty to defining love. How do you define love? I don't think you can. The old Scotsman had it right when he said, "It's better felt than telt.'"

With no scriptural definition, the best we can do is describe how it operates without being too specific. In many ways, learning to worship is similar to learning to love. It is something that happens in your heart. Most people don't need a manual to learn how to love someone. They don't need a step-by-step explanation on how to work up loving emotions. No, love is a spontaneous action. In the same way, worship is a spontaneous action, too.

Expressions of Love

Even though love can't be defined, it *must* be expressed. I've done a lot of counseling in my life. Many times the bottom line for the wives who come for counseling is that they feel their husbands don't love them anymore. But when I would tell the husband, "Your wife feels that you don't love her anymore," he would be shocked. And invariably, when you get right down to it, a major problem in such marriages is the husband's inability to express to his wife that he loves her.

We live in a culture, especially in North America, where it is difficult for some of us to really express what we feel in our hearts towards someone else. If you find it hard to express your feelings in your relationships with people, you are also going to find it difficult as you come into the presence of God.

Breaking Through the Barriers

Your reluctance to express the passion and love of your heart will stop you from embracing the Lord and moving in to where He is, into the power of His presence. If you're going to worship God, that is one thing you've got to be willing to do. You've got to be willing to let the barriers down and to throw yourself in adoration upon the Lord.

I was raised in a home where we really didn't use phrases like, "I love you," a whole lot. I don't think I heard it more than five times in all my early life from my parents. It was just something that was not done. We didn't express deep and intense emotions. Shirley and I have made a commitment to turn that around in our home. We express our love to each other and to the children all the time.

This was not easy for me at first. Because of my conservative background, I was reluctant to express the passion of my heart openly. That same difficulty created problems when I desired to worship God because I had difficulty breaking down the barriers and really telling the Lord how passionately I loved Him and how I felt about Him. *Most of us don't worship well because we have a problem with intimacy.*

A Response to a Relationship

Worship is intense intimacy. It is an expression of love that releases all of your heart's adoration, it releases your mind's determination and it releases the strength of your body to worship the Lord with your whole heart.

Worship primarily is a response to a relationship. Said another way, your relationship to God is expressed by worship. If you love somebody, you will want to hug and kiss them as an expression of the way you feel, but if you don't love somebody, hugging and kissing them won't necessarily cause love to grow. The hugs and kisses are an expression of something you have inside, not a performance you do to stir up love.

That is why praise cannot manufacture worship for you. Thanksgiving cannot manufacture worship for you. You don't stir worship up. Worship is an attitude of your heart that is there because you love God, because of what God has done for you. It is an expression of the way you feel toward Him for what He's done. *We love Him because He first loved us.*

I can't "perform" worship by clapping, or singing, or crying, or dancing. You don't make yourself worship by doing any one of these things. Rather, when you love God, you are going to worship Him. And when you worship Him, you may sing, you may clap, you may dance, or you may be absolutely silent and do nothing. Each individual has his own unique response.

The Divine Spark

It is so important for you to see that it is the presence of God that actually creates worship. I can teach you to pray, and I can teach you to sing. I can teach you to give thanksgiving. I can even teach you to praise, but I cannot teach you to worship. That is between you and your God, because worship is your individual response to the presence of God. You are the only one who can initiate it through the power of the Holy Spirit.

It is as intangible as love. You cannot teach anybody how to love. If conditions are right, they do it naturally. It is an expression of the heart toward another person. Worship is the expression of your spirit toward Almighty God. You cannot teach anybody how to worship, but when conditions are right, it happens. You know when the worship is there and so does God. Praise will bring you into God's presence, but worship is what you do once you reach His presence.

Have you ever walked across the room in the wintertime when it is dry and cold and then kissed someone? Remember what happens? When you're just about to kiss, a spark jumps the gap, and you both get a shock.

In a sense, that is what happens when we pass from praise into worship. You are praising the Lord, you are thanking Him for who He is, when all of a sudden, the words of your mouth move to an attitude of the heart. Love wells up, and adoration comes exploding out of your innermost being. There's a snap: it's almost as though the lips were touching. Excuse the intimacy of my description, but there is no better way to say it. There's that snap, and when the snap comes, the electricity is there.

All of a sudden, you know you are where He is. There is an awesome sense now: *God is here, He is around you. This is worship.* You may cry, you may dance, you may clap, you may fall to your knees, you may be absolutely quiet, but the presence of God is there *and you know it.* You *are* worshiping.

That's why it's impossible to legislate worship. I cannot tell you what to do when you worship, that is the response of your heart to your Maker, to Almighty God. You do it the way you feel that God tells you to do it. It's an individual matter.

There are times at night, after Shirley has gone to sleep, when I worship. Just meditating on the Word and the blood brings me into the presence of God. Sometimes I weep openly. Sometimes I raise my hands with an inexpressible sense of the presence of God exploding inside me. I don't make any noise at all, so as not to awaken my wife. Some of these sessions have gone on for several hours. What a refreshing I receive from the Lord!

God Seeks True Worship

The thing God wants from us, more than anything else, is our worship. Yet, when someone receives Christ in the average church, rather than teaching the new convert how to worship, the first thing we teach him is how to work. We press him into the service of the church. We spend a whole lot of time training him to be a worker rather than to be a worshiper. Yet, the thing God wants most from us is our worship, not our service.

Remember when the devil offered Jesus all the kingdoms of the world if He would fall down and worship him? Jesus said, in Matthew 4:10, *"Thou shalt worship the Lord thy God, and him only shalt thou serve."* Worship is first, and service comes second. Don't make a worker out of somebody: make him or her a worshiper first, and the service will follow from the act of worship.

Being a worshiper first and foremost will bring everything we do into the realm of service. Paul writes, *"Whatsoever ye do, do it heartily, as to the Lord, and not unto men....for ye serve the Lord Christ"* (Col. 3:23-24). Worship will bring all our service into the Kingdom of God.

Choose the Better Part

It is true worship that God seeks. That's why Jesus commended Mary. Remember the story? Martha was busy in the kitchen, doing the work, while Mary was sitting at the feet of Jesus, feasting on the words He had to say. Did you ever wonder why Jesus rebuked Martha when she said, "Jesus, tell Mary to get up and come on in here to the kitchen and help me." She was the server, she was the working kind. Mary just sat there worshiping.

Jesus said, "Martha, relax. Mary has chosen the better part. She is doing the right thing. She is here basking in the presence of God. That is what I want, and that is what she needs."

We get so busy in the work of God, and so active, running here and there. The biggest joy of my life is taking time out to be with God, to just sit and to be where He is, to bask in His presence, and to give Him the expression and the adoration and the passion of my heart. It takes time to do that. Most of us are so tied up in the hustle and bustle of life, we don't want to take the time. In the process, we miss out on the most wonderful opportunity of our lives.

An Example of Worship

There is a classic example of worship given to us in the Scriptures that beautifully illustrates the principles we have been studying. Luke 7:36 records the occasion when Jesus was invited to eat at the home of a Pharisee named Simon:

And one of the Pharisees desired him that he would eat with him. And he went into the Pharisee's house, and sat down to meat. And, behold, a woman in the city, which was a sinner, when she knew that Jesus sat at meat in the Pharisee's house, brought an alabaster box of ointment, And stood at his feet behind him weeping, and began to wash his feet with tears,

and did wipe them with the hairs of her head, and kissed his feet, and anointed them with the ointment. Now when the Pharisee which had bidden him saw it, he spake within himself, saying, This man, if he were a prophet, would have known who and what manner of woman this is that toucheth him, for she is a sinner.

This is an extremely powerful illustration of worship. Here is what worship does. This is a picture of a true worshiping heart. It's interesting to note that this woman, a sinner, a street prostitute, understood worship better than the religious man who had spent all of his life in the synagogue.

There is something we can learn here. Just because you have been going to church for thirty years does not mean that you know how to worship. Here is a woman, a street prostitute, who was forgiven the degradation of her sin. She knew what brokenness was, and she knew what worship was. Yet the religious man, the Pharisee, sat and criticized her for what she did. That goes on in churches all over the nation all the time.

This woman wept and washed the feet of Jesus. She kissed His feet again and again. This is the attitude that produces worship. Let me describe this to you. First of all, notice the brokenness, the tears. Tears have a way of cleansing your heart and getting rid of the imperfections.

She knows that she has nothing to be proud of. She knows her mistakes — in fact, the whole town knows her mistakes! Everybody in that room knew she was a sinner when she walked in. They all knew who she was. She had no righteousness of her own; she was a sinner and she knew it. She came in, and with tears, she washed Jesus' feet. Remember what David said, *"The sacrifices of God are a broken spirit: a broken and a contrite heart, O God, thou wilt not despise"* (Ps. 51:17).

I want you to notice another thing about this woman — her humility. She began to wash Jesus' feet with her tears, and she wiped them with her hair. Without an insight into the customs of the time, the full impact of this can slip right past us. Paul declares that a woman's long hair was her glory; it was her covering. In Jesus' day, a woman wore a covering over her head to show that she was under the authority of a man, or under a man's covering, much as a woman today would wear a wedding ring.

In this story, the woman let her hair down in the presence of Jesus. Every man in that room was electrified when they saw her do it. That was what a wife did when she was about to go to bed with her husband. That's what a prostitute did when she was about to seduce a stranger. She would let her hair down.

What an incredible display of emotion! She didn't care what they thought. She was there to lavish the love of her heart on Jesus. This was not a sexual thing; this was a worship experience from the heart. She wept, and she let her hair down, an intimate act that outraged every man in that room. To think that she would come in and do that to Jesus! She knew what they thought, but she didn't care. She had come to give everything of herself to Him because of who He was.

Then this woman took her hair and she wiped Jesus' dusty feet, that had been made muddy with her own tears. Remember Paul says a woman's hair is her glory — she takes her glory to wipe His feet. What a powerful picture. When you come to Jesus, when you come to God, you come without pride. You come with humility. That is the true spirit of worship.

The Alabaster Box

The woman brought an alabaster box full of precious ointment. Most unmarried women hoarded their life's savings in order to buy this ointment, which they would store in an alabaster box. Mark 14:3-9 records the story of how Mary of Bethany anointed Jesus with precious ointment just before the Last Supper. The Bible declares that the ointment she put on Jesus was worth a full year's wages. That is how valuable that ointment was.

We can assume that the ointment this woman is putting on Jesus' feet was her dowry. It was what a woman gave to her husband in marriage. She was sacrificing her future. She was giving everything she had. She was lavishing it on Jesus. Why?

If you are a true worshiper, a desire will come to your heart to give to God in some way or another. You are going to want to give your time, you are going to want to give your devotion, you are going to want to give your money. The Old Testament says, *"Thou shalt not appear before the Lord empty handed"* (Deut. 16:16, TAB). Giving generously is a sign of true worship.

After this woman had finished washing the feet of Jesus, she broke her alabaster box. She had to break it; that was the only way the perfumed ointment could flow out. In like manner, some of us keep our emotions stored up in an alabaster box. We need to break the protective walls that surround our feelings, so we can let them flow out and lavish them on the Lord.

Who Loves Most?

Remember, all this was happening in the house of Simon, the Pharisee, the proud religious keeper of the Law. A street woman has come into his house and has let down her hair in the presence of his guests. She has been washing and kissing Jesus' feet. Simon is thinking in his heart, "How can this Jesus be a prophet? He obviously does not know how bad this woman is, and how suggestive this action is, that she has let down her hair in my house and in the presence of this Man."

Simon was horrified and upset. Sometimes we have a way of judging others because we don't think we have sinned as badly as they have. I want to suggest something to you. There is no degree to sin. You are either a sinner or you are not a sinner. You may be an upstanding member of your community while your neighbor is a prostitute: your sin may not be the same as hers, but you are a sinner nonetheless. And sin is sin.

At this point, Jesus said something very significant. He said, *"Her sins, which are many, are forgiven; for she loved much, but to whom little is forgiven, the same loveth little. And he said unto her, Thy sins are forgiven"* (Luke 7:47). The woman had poured out her heart on Jesus, and He forgave her sins. I tell you, when you truly worship the Lord, the sin problem is taken care of automatically. Praise God!

Then Jesus spoke to Simon and rebuked him. He said, "Simon, you don't think you've been forgiven very much because you're so good. So you don't love very much. This woman knows she has been forgiven a whole lot and that is why she loves so intensely."

The Measure of Your Worship

The measure of your worship relates directly to how badly you know you need the grace of God. You need to realize what a sinner you have been and what the grace of God has done in lifting you up. It's possible to lose the power of worship because we have lost sight of how abhorrent our personal sin was in the eyes of Almighty God.

I have seen the ugliness of my own personal sin. I know my sin put Jesus on the cross. It was my sin that killed Him. And I would suggest to you that until you see this, you will never appreciate your redemption. Your sin put Him on that cross. Your sin killed Him!

Once I have seen that it was my sin that killed Jesus, only then can I become contrite like this woman. Otherwise, I become proud of who I am. I become proud of my reputation. I become proud of my spiritual brownie points and what I've done for God. This is a stench in the nostrils of God. A person who is full of pride cannot worship. That is the Pharisee amongst us, and everyone of us must beware of it. Everyone of us is prone to Phariseeism, to self-righteousness, if we do not examine ourselves constantly.

When you come and worship, don't come in the pride of the flesh. It simply won't work. Rather, come knowing that even though you were a sinner, you have been given the opportunity to actually be in the presence of the holy God. The implications of that are absolutely awesome.

The Spirit of Adoption

If I were to stand in the measure of the merits of Terry Law, I would have no right to be declaring the Gospel of Jesus Christ to you. I have made too many mistakes; I have fallen flat on my face time after time after time.

But one day God reached down and touched my heart with His love. He said, *"I want you to be my son. I'm going to give you the gift of righteousness. I am going to cleanse you with the blood of my Son. I am going to make you my child. I am going to take away the spirit of bondage, and I am going to give you the spirit of adoption."*

When Shirley and I married, she had two children; I had three. We made a decision that we would adopt each other's children. We went to a judge, and the judge asked the children if they wanted to be adopted in this way. The children said, "Yes, we do," and we signed the legal documents.

The birth certificates for our children now declare that Shirley is the legal mother of my children. The birth certificates declare that I am the legal father of her children. In the eyes of the law, in the eyes of the world, and in the eyes of our children, we are now their true mother and father.

Adoption is an awesome thing. We have not been given the spirit of bondage again to fear, but we have been given the spirit of adoption. Jesus is my elder brother. God is my Father. I am His child. That makes me want to worship. That makes me want to bless the Lord.

Worship Produces Faith

The next thing Jesus said to the woman was, *"Thy faith hath saved thee"* (Luke 7:50). Do you know what worship does? Worship will automatically create faith. I have found that people who truly know how to worship are the people who get healed the easiest. You see, faith automatically runs concurrent with the worshiping spirit, because a worshiping spirit is not founded in self-righteousness.

The hardest people to get healed are the self-righteous ones, the ones who think they deserve it, the ones who wonder why in the world God hasn't healed them after they have been serving Him for so many years. They are precisely the ones who don't get it because they don't realize they were just as bad a sinner as anybody else, and it is the grace of God that has given them righteousness.

This street prostitute came to Jesus, and Jesus said to her, *"Your faith has saved you."* Her worship created faith. Faith is automatically there in the heart of a true worshiper.

That is why, if I can lead an audience in praise and get them to move toward worship, as they proceed toward worship, the electric power of healing will be in the audience. One Sunday morning in a church in Boise, Idaho, I was leading people into high praise when all of a sudden the snap took place and I sensed we were in the actual manifest presence of God. The glory was there.

Have you ever been in the presence of the glory of God? It is an awesome thing when you get there. I opened my eyes after we had been there for perhaps half an hour, and I couldn't see the audience. Some of them were lying on the floor, some of them were on their knees. Nobody told them what to do: God was there.

A young woman of sixteen was sitting at the back; she had been born deaf in both ears. In the middle of that atmosphere, faith was generated, and her ears opened up, and the sound came on as if somebody had turned on a radio. She was healed in both ears instantly. She came running to the front to get right with God. Hallelujah! Faith was there in the midst of worship.

Jesus said, *"Thy faith hath saved thee...."* The word *saved,* as it appears there, comes from the Greek *sozo.* It means deliverance. Your faith has given you all the benefits of God, all the goodness of God, all the blessings of God, all the prosperity of God. His righteousness, His healing, and His abundance flow to the worshiper. They are our rightful inheritance as His child. Nothing, nothing, nothing draws the heart of God towards you like your worship.

Go in Peace

The last thing Jesus told the woman was, *"Go in peace."* Worship brings faith, deliverance, and then finally, peace. Let me tell you, if you have a stress problem, you need to worship God. The peace of God that passes understanding comes to you as you worship. Your problems suddenly seem small in comparison with the Father's power, His tender love for you, and His willingness to use His power on your behalf. A few moments with your Father in worship will take care of the stress and give you peace.

For This You Were Created!

The pattern for the high priest to proceed into the presence of God is very significant for us today. Every stop along the way has been designed by God to prepare you for this moment: your sin has been dealt with at the altar of brass, the dust of life is washed away at the brazen laver. At the table of showbread, you submit your will to God, and you quiet the objections of your mind at the golden candlestick. Now you offer your heart-felt praise at the altar of incense. Suddenly, there's that divine snap, that moment of electricity happens, and you sense the awesome presence of God. With your whole being, you reach out to God, and your feel His power, love, acceptance, and blessings flowing to you.

> ***There is no other joy or peace like this.***
> ***For this you were created!***

ACKNOWLEDGMENTS

I would like to gratefully acknowledge Derek Prince for his tape series, *The Way Into the Holiest,* and Judson Cornwall for his book, *Let Us Worship.*

Steps to Enter the Presence of God

1. **ENTER HIS GATES** with thanksgiving (Ps. 100:4). Remember what God has done for you in the past. This builds faith, and starts moving you toward the presence of God.

2. At **THE BRAZEN ALTAR,** we deal with our sin and overcome guilt. Confess your sins and experience God's forgiveness (1 John 1:9).

   Declare the power of the blood of Jesus to completely remove all trace of sin:

   "According to Ephesians 1:7, by the blood of Jesus, I am redeemed, bought back, out of the hand of the devil; all my sins are completely forgiven right now. They have been remitted."

   "According to Romans 5:9, by the blood of Jesus, I am justified, I am made righteous, just as if I had never sinned."

   "According to Hebrews 13:12, by the blood of Jesus, I am sanctified, made holy, set apart unto God."

   "According to 1 Peter 2:24, by His stripes I was healed. If I was healed at the cross, then I am healed now. Sickness and disease, you have no place in me. I am healed by His blood."

   "According to 1 Corinthians 6:19-20, my body is the temple of the Holy Ghost, redeemed, forgiven, cleansed, made righteous, sanctified, and healed by the blood of Jesus. Therefore, Satan has no place in me. He has no power over me. I renounce him. I loose myself from him by the power of the blood of Jesus."

   Acknowledge that your sin nature died with Jesus when He was crucified. You were crucified with Christ and are no longer a slave to sin (Rom. 6:6).

   Dedicate yourself as a living sacrifice to God for service (Rom. 12:1).

3. **THE BRAZEN LAVER** is the place to lay aside troubles, cares, and fears. Spend time reading and meditating on the Word of God. Let it wash you. Experience rest, relaxation, refreshing and

renewal as you receive God's Word.

4. **ENTER THE HOLY PLACE** with praise. Move beyond thanking God for the many good things He has done for you, and begin to magnify His character and His loving nature which are behind all His actions. Praise Him for His love, mercy, power, grace, longsuffering, and lovingkindness. Praise is not based on how you feel, but on your decision to "bless the Lord at all times" (Ps. 34:1).

4. At **THE TABLE OF SHOWBREAD,** you submit your will to God and His plan. Decide to think God's thoughts and willingly do what He says to do. Say, "Father, today I am going to serve you. My will is going to be obedient to yours."

5. **THE GOLDEN CANDLESTICK** is where you win the battle of the mind. Tell your mind to be quiet, and stop thinking the devil's thoughts (2 Cor. 10:5). Renew your mind according to the Word of God (Rom. 12:2). Stop listening to what the world says and what your senses say, and start picking up what your spirit is saying. Pray in the spirit, interpret back. Determine to obey the instructions the Holy Spirit gives you.

6. You release your emotions at **THE GOLDEN ALTAR OF INCENSE.** Express your love to God: remember he who has been forgiven much loves much (Luke 7:41-47). Let the barriers down and throw yourself in adoration upon the Lord. Don't let your reluctance to express your emotions keep you from moving into the presence of God.

7. In **THE HOLY OF HOLIES,** you will experience the presence of God. Worship in Spirit, and sense His holiness. Nothing draws the heart of God towards you like your worship. Enjoy fullness of joy in His presence, then go in peace. Your problems will suddenly seem small in comparison with the Father's power, His tender love for you, and His willingness to use His power in your behalf.

About the Author
TERRY LAW

FOR OVER 25 YEARS, Terry Law has obeyed the call to take God's Word to communist nations. In the 1970's, Terry and his international missionary team, Living Sound, took gospel music into the former USSR. In the early 1980's, he smuggled tape-duplicating equipment behind the Iron Curtain and began duplicating New Testaments in Russian for secret distribution through the unregistered churches.

Since 1990, Terry has given away over 4.5 million Bibles and New Testaments and thirteen million copies of *The Story of Jesus* and *Your New Life* booklets in the former Soviet Union.

In 1994, Terry visited both China and Cuba, and arranged to provide Bibles, New Testaments, and gospel literature to these two communist nations as well.

In addition to meeting the spiritual needs of people in the countries where he ministers, Terry has been moved by compassion to help meet their physical needs as well, acting as a channel to provide food and basic medicines to children's hospitals, Bible schools, and even to the war zones.

For a complete catalog of tapes and books by Terry Law, write to:
Law Outreach Ministries
P.O. Box 3563
Tulsa, Oklahoma 74101

Books by Terry Law
Available From Victory House

Praise Releases Faith

The Power of Praise and Worship

How to Enter the Presence of God

How to Overcome Guilt

Victory House, Inc.
P.O. Box 700238 • Tulsa, OK 74170